MORE VEGETABLE~~~~~SE

Delicious Vegetable Side Dishes
for Everyday Meals

by Janet Fletcher
Photography by
Keith Ovregaard

An Astolat Book
HARLOW & RATNER
Emeryville, California

Food Styling: **Susan Massey-Weil**
Prop Styling: **Debbie Dicker**
Illustrations: **Susan Mattmann**
Typography: **Classic Typography**
Design and Production: **Schuettge & Carleton**

Props for photography: Cedanna, San Francisco (pgs. 154, 195)
Columbine, Corte Madera (pgs. 32, 62, 122, 140, 163, 177, 184, 218)
Sue Fisher King, San Francisco (pgs. 62, 118, 204, 211)
Holly Hartley, Mill Valley (pg. 138)
Gary Holt, Berkeley (pg. 204)
Karen Winograde, Napa (pg. 154)

Cover photo: Baked Ratatouille; recipe page 84

Library of Congress Cataloging-in-Publication Data

Fletcher, Janet Kessel.
    More vegetables, please : delicious vegetable side dishes for
everyday meals / by Janet Fletcher ; photography by Keith Ovregaard.
        p.   cm.
    "An Astolat book."
    Includes index.
    ISBN 0–9627345–3–5 : $16.95
    1. Cookery (Vegetables)   2. Side dishes (cookery)   I. Ovregaard,
Keith.   II. Title.
TX801.F56   1992
641.6′5—dc20   92–15605
                                                                          CIP

Printed in Hong Kong
10 9 8 7 6 5 4 3 2 1

Harlow & Ratner
5749 Landregan Street
Emeryville, CA 94608

CONTENTS

ACKNOWLEDGMENTS

I'd like to express my thanks to several people who contributed significantly to this book. I am grateful to Jay Harlow and Elaine Ratner, whose idea it was and who gave me the forum to share my enthusiasm for vegetables. I am also indebted to Elaine for her sensitive and thoughtful editing. Two of the best cooks I know, Niloufer Ichaporia and Sharon Thomas, shared recipes and techniques from their own kitchens. The United Fresh Fruit and Vegetable Association and Bess Petlak of Frieda's, Inc. provided valuable information about specific vegetables. I also want to thank the talented team who made this book beautiful: food stylist Susan Massey-Weil, photo stylist Debbie Dicker, photographer Keith Ovregaard, and illustrator Susan Mattmann. Above all, I must acknowledge the loving support of my husband Doug, who good-naturedly ate recipe tests for dinner every night for a long time.

INTRODUCTION

Raised on canned and frozen vegetables, I couldn't believe the produce markets I saw when I moved to California for college. They overflowed with vegetables my mother had never prepared: fresh artichokes, fresh asparagus, fresh beets, fresh peas. And there were vegetables I'd hardly seen, let alone tasted: rutabagas, fennel, kale, parsnips, fava beans. A professional interest in cooking blossomed with that move to California and, with it, a passion for vegetables.

In the intervening years, I've prepared a wide variety of vegetables in hundreds of ways. I've learned how they taste, how best to cook them, how to enhance them with herbs and spices, how to pair them with other vegetables. And I've discovered that guests delight in vegetables presented in unexpected ways, that an enticing vegetable side dish can light up a menu.

I'm not alone in this discovery. In the decade I've been reviewing San Francisco Bay Area restaurants, I've witnessed major shifts in restaurant food. Restaurants are finding that it pays to pay attention to vegetables. In the old-style restaurants, chefs put all their time into the "center of the plate"—the meat or fish—and gave little thought to the accompanying vegetables; every plate would come out of the kitchen with the same rice pilaf and soggy zucchini. Now chefs are realizing that creatively presented vegetables can heighten a main course's appeal. Rice and steamed zucchini are giving way to such inviting accompaniments as corn cakes, garlic mashed potatoes, Jerusalem artichoke gratin, fava beans with chicory and mint, eggplant fritters, leek and mushroom ragout, fried okra, couscous with artichokes—all side dishes I've encountered on restaurant menus lately.

Expanding your vegetable repertoire will pay dividends at home too. Your meals will be more varied and thus more enjoyable to cook and to eat. Too many cooks allow themselves to get in a vegetable rut, always preparing green beans or broccoli in the same one or two ways. Small wonder that both cook and eaters lose interest. New combinations and new flavors can reawaken your own and your family's interest in vegetables that have become too familiar.

You'll also find that meals take less time to prepare when you give vegetables a little more thought. With an imaginative side dish, you don't need anything more elaborate than a broiled lamb chop, a baked fish fillet, or a roast chicken. Let the vegetable provide that element of the unexpected, and keep the meat simple.

You can save money, too, when you elevate the status of vegetables—even when you buy top-quality produce. I know I pay a lot more for beautiful, slender green beans at a specialty market than I would pay for ordinary beans at a supermarket, but I think it's economical. The beans are so delicious that we eat a lot of them and a little meat, and meat costs more per serving than fancy beans do. I find that people

5

are satisfied with a small meat portion when the vegetables are enticing. In fact, they're grateful, because almost everyone these days is trying to cut back on meat and eat more vegetables.

Do you have reluctant vegetable eaters in your family? Appetizing side dishes will win them over and make your meals more healthful. After all, there's no nutrition in a vegetable that people won't eat. When you take the time to prepare vegetables too enticing to resist, you are doing yourself and your family a favor. Vegetables are our main dietary source of vitamins; many also provide significant minerals and fiber. Most are low in sodium or sodium-free. Although there's no explaining the quirky tastes of children, a vegetable that looks and smells appetizing is going to stand a better chance of acceptance than the same old tired squash.

At home my husband and I often make a whole meal of side dishes. We don't do so for health reasons; we do it because the vegetables are so delicious and satisfying. Nevertheless, the health benefits are hard to ignore. I have no doubt that our frequent all-vegetable meals help us, despite our food-related professions, to keep our weight under control. Eating more vegetables leaves less room for empty calories. What's more, many fresh-picked vegetables contain natural sugar which causes them to strike the palate with a subtle or not-so-subtle sweetness. I think one reason I don't have much taste for desserts is that my large appetite for vegetables satisfies my "sweet tooth."

I also love the way vegetable side dishes reflect and celebrate the seasons. It's automatically a special dinner when I bring home the year's first asparagus, or the first vine-ripened tomatoes, or the first sweet corn. For me, the sense of anticipation adds tremendous pleasure to the table and thus to my daily life.

When I learned how much better vegetables can taste at peak season, I learned the most important lesson for a vegetable cook. You can't take overgrown, bitter zucchini and make a tasty side dish, no matter how much you fuss; but when you have young, firm, sweet zucchini, you don't need to do much to them to make them delicious. The best-tasting vegetable dishes start with the best vegetables. That's one reason I have become such an enthusiastic gardener and recommend it to anyone who can make the time and the space. No potatoes will ever taste as good as the thin-skinned new potatoes you dig in your own backyard; no peas will be as sweet as those you pick off the vine and cook that night. Here in California, the produce basket of the nation, I can readily buy many vegetables as good as the ones I can grow; if you can't, I encourage you to discover the satisfaction of growing your own.

In the following pages, cooks looking for inspiration will find more than 200 answers to the "What should I serve with the roast" dilemma. As one who loves vegetables and vegetable cooking, I could imagine a book with 800 vegetable dishes. Since space doesn't allow me to be comprehensive, I have tried to be representative, offering a variety of techniques and ideas that can be applied to a variety of vegetables. The recipes often suggest other vegetables that will work using the same techniques.

In selecting and refining my favorite vegetable dishes, I kept in mind that time and health are major concerns for many cooks these days. With few exceptions, the recipes in this book are easy and quick to prepare; many can be made in a single pot. And I've kept fat to a minimum. Nevertheless, some wonderful side dishes do require more than a few minutes, more than a single pot, and/or more fat than some diets permit. You can avoid those few, but I include them unapologetically, knowing that the delicious results will repay the expenditure in time and calories.

I hope this book awakens or strengthens your enthusiasm for vegetables. In my eyes, they're a gift of the soil and the seasons, with infinite possibilities. I hope that you, too, will come to look at vegetables as opportunities for creativity. And while you build your own repertoire, I hope my recipes make your kitchen a more enjoyable place and your dinner table continually inviting.

Janet Fletcher
Oakland, California, 1992

A VEGETABLE PRIMER

COOKING WITH THE SEASONS

All vegetables used to have seasons. Now, thanks to sophisticated controlled-atmosphere storage, refrigerated shipping, and the stepped-up exports of southern hemisphere growers, Americans can get almost anything almost any time of year.

Nevertheless, I cling to the old-fashioned idea of seasonality. You can get tomatoes every month of the year, but you get the best tomatoes when your local growers are harvesting. When vegetables aren't in season in your area, they have to come from farther away—often from Mexico or Florida or other warm climates. They have to be picked underripe to withstand shipping, so their flavor isn't fully developed. Or, as is the case with corn and peas, the vegetables lose sweetness in the several days it takes to get them to you. Vegetables shipped from across the world, or even across the country, are rarely as good as vegetables grown near you, picked at peak flavor, and on your table within a day or two.

I would rather do without tomatoes until the vine-ripened beauties arrive in summer; the rest of the year you pay a premium price for lesser quality. Besides, some pleasures are sweeter for having to wait for them; the anticipation makes the local tomatoes taste even better. Cook with the seasons and you will spend less, eat better, and enjoy it more.

To help you, I have arranged the recipes in this book by season, based on the dominant vegetables in each dish. In my mind, a vegetable's season is the time when the domestic crop is at its peak of quantity and quality. A special all-seasons chapter includes those produce items that are available in good supply and good condition year-round.

Clearly this organizational scheme isn't airtight. Some vegetables span seasons and some dishes, especially those containing several vegetables, could arguably be attributed to more than one season. Then there are "cusp" dishes like Autumn Squash and Corn (page 130) that pair a late summer vegetable with an early autumn one. For guidance, I turned to the Supply Guide provided by the United Fresh Fruit and Vegetable Association (UFFVA), which indicates what percentage of a particular crop comes on the nation's wholesale market in each month. Broccoli, for example, is in reasonably good supply year-round, but the UFFVA figures show that it's slightly more plentiful in winter—so in the winter chapter it goes. If you don't find a vegetable or a dish where you expect it to be, please check the index.

IF YOU CAN'T SHOP OFTEN, SHOP WISELY

To make delicious side dishes, you need good raw materials. Even the best recipes won't taste good if your peas are starchy, your broccoli old and strong, or your tomatoes as hard as baseballs.

How do you recognize quality? Within the seasonal chapters I've given specific guidelines for each vegetable, but I can also offer some general advice.

Quality—which to me means good taste—in produce is a function of many factors: the particular variety selected and the soil and climate in which it is grown; farming practices; harvest procedures; and post-harvest packing, shipping, and handling. You don't have to know any of those details, however, because your senses can be your guide. Some vegetables turn a particular color when ripe, some develop a pleasing aroma, others have a certain surface feel or texture. Learn to trust your senses, especially your common sense. You know almost instinctively that limp zucchini, hard tomatoes, wilted spinach, and spongy eggplants aren't going to taste good.

Some aspects of quality aren't intuitive, however. Despite the visual allure of beefsteak tomatoes and artichokes as big as softballs, bigger vegetables aren't always better. In fact, the reverse is more often true. As most vegetables grow, their tissue becomes more fibrous, woodier, or tougher; their flavor gets stronger or less sweet. Leafy greens get tougher; cabbage family vegetables get stronger in flavor; squash and cucumbers get seedier and more watery. That's why so many chefs seek out baby vegetables—tiny carrots, turnips, beets the size of marbles, and zucchini no bigger than a finger. Unfortunately, some growers have taken that idea too far, offering vegetables picked so young that they haven't developed any flavor yet. Bigger isn't often better, but smaller has its limits, too.

In the San Francisco Bay Area, we are blessed with many farmers' markets and small produce markets that buy directly from local growers. I prefer those two sources to supermarkets. In my experience, supermarkets tend to value appearance, shelf life, consistent supply, and low price over taste. Specialty produce markets may be more expensive than supermarkets, but I consider it a false economy to try to save pennies on produce that doesn't taste good.

Ideally, you have a wonderful produce market near you where you can conveniently stop every day; realistically, that's probably not the case. Many people can't find time to market more than once a week, and many don't have a first-rate market near them.

Flexibility is one solution to the latter problem. Be willing to alter your menu to take advantage of whatever vegetable looks best when you shop. If the broccoli is limp and yellowing, check out the cabbage or the brussels sprouts. If the store has a fresh shipment of just-picked corn, take advantage of it.

If you can't shop often, shop wisely when you do. Buy a variety of vegetables and plan meals to incorporate the most perishable ones early in the week, the least perishable ones later. For each of the vegetables featured in this book, I've given storage guidelines and an estimate of how long you can expect the item to stay in good condition, but here's a rough-and-ready chart to help you:

Highly Perishable
   (use within 1 to 2 days of purchase)

asparagus	mushrooms
broccoli	okra
brussels sprouts	peas
corn	

Somewhat Perishable
   (use within 2 to 3 days of purchase)

artichokes	green or yellow snap beans
chard	greens for cooking
cucumbers	spinach
eggplant	summer squash
fava beans	

Fairly Good Keepers
   (use within 4 to 7 days of purchase)

cardoon	Jerusalem artichokes
carrots	leeks
celery root	sweet peppers
fennel	tomatoes (use faster if fully ripe)

Very Good Keepers
   (will keep 1 week or more)

beets	potatoes
cabbage	rutabagas
hard squash	sweet potatoes
onions	turnips
parsnips	

Is fresh always better? In my eyes, the answer is no. Fresh peas, in particular, are often a disappointment. Harold McGee, author of *On Food and Cooking* (Charles Scribner's Sons, 1984), says that peas lose up to 40 percent of their sugar in six hours at room temperature. Unless you buy peas at a farmers' market or grow them yourself, you may find that frozen petite peas are sweeter and more tender than what's available fresh. I think they are a shining example of a tasty frozen vegetable. Lima beans are another. Frozen baby limas are delicious, to my taste, and fresh limas are hard to find.

Those are the only two frozen vegetables that I use, however. I would rather cook something else than substitute frozen artichokes, frozen green beans, or frozen broccoli for fresh.

Canned vegetables are even less successful than frozen ones, in my opinion. With the exception of canned tomatoes, I don't use them.

STORING VEGETABLES

When you get back from the market, take a few extra minutes to store your vegetables properly; it will prolong their useful life and, in the long run, save you time and money.

To prepare vegetables for storage, discard any wilted or yellowing leaves or decaying parts. If you've bought carrots with tops, cut them off and discard them. Beet greens or turnip greens that are still attached to the roots should be cut off and stored separately, otherwise the leaves will continue to draw moisture from the roots.

Most vegetables purchased at a market have already been washed and don't need further washing before storage. Home-grown vegetables should be scrubbed clean before storing.

Most vegetables like to be kept in a humid environment to prevent moisture loss. (Among the exceptions are onions, potatoes, sweet potatoes, eggplant, okra, tomatoes, mushrooms, and hard-skinned squashes.) The vegetable crisper in your refrigerator is designed with that in mind; because it's a small, confined space, it has higher humidity than the main refrigerator compartment. On the other hand, water condensing on the surface of most vegetables encourages mold. For that reason, I store most vegetables in the crisper in a perforated plastic bag—a bag that I punch holes in to allow air circulation. Leafy greens don't have to be stored in a bag—they can be put directly in the crisper—but they will wilt a little faster without one. If your crisper is full and you must put vegetables in the main compartment, be sure to put them in a perforated plastic bag to prevent moisture loss. A paper bag, which many people prefer to plastic, will also help prevent moisture loss; however, I suspect that paper, being more porous, doesn't work quite as well. I'm not aware of any controlled experiments on that subject.

PLANNING A MENU

In a satisfying meal, the parts complement each other. Every vegetable dish should flatter the meat or other main dish it accompanies.

But how do you know what goes with what? In the introduction to each recipe in this book, you'll find my suggestions for companion meat dishes. Sometimes the choice is pure common sense—like putting an unsauced meat or fish with a "saucy" side dish, recommending an Italian main course for an Italian-style vegetable, or proposing a delicate fish to accompany a delicate side dish. With some preparations, it's a matter of taste. I don't generally like cheese with fish, for example, so you won't find me recommending salmon for a side dish garnished with Parmesan.

In general, aim for contrasting textures and colors. Serve a dark creamy puree, like Old-Fashioned Creamed Spinach (page 186), with a pale chicken breast; match soft and juicy Baked Tomatoes with Feta (page 111) with a firm grilled steak. Flavors should be compatible but not repetitious. If the meat has tomato, tarragon, or cream in it, the vegetable shouldn't. I also try to match styles—putting a "homey" dish like Root Vegetable Hash (page 180) with a humble pot roast. And I rarely mix ethnic ideas on one plate. If the side dish has Asian seasonings like ginger and fresh coriander, I go with a meat that has Asian flavors, too.

Imagine what the finished plate will look and taste like. Is it eye-appealing? Are you tempted by the combination? If so, then it's probably right.

Remember to consider kitchen logistics when deciding what vegetable dish to make. If you have only one oven and you've planned to roast chicken for dinner, you'll need a side dish that bakes at the same temperature as the chicken, or you'll need to make your side dish on top of the stove. Don't overcrowd your oven; putting dishes too close together will hamper air circulation so that nothing cooks properly.

Issues of timing are also important. If your meat takes some last-minute attention, select a vegetable dish that doesn't. I don't like to disappear into the kitchen for long stretches when we have guests, so I plan accordingly, choosing braised or baked side dishes and avoiding sautes.

SERVING IT FORTH

I'm particular about the temperature at which I serve foods. When foods are very hot or very cold, it's hard to taste them. With some dishes—especially braised or baked dishes that contain a lot of ingredients—the flavors don't meld until the dish has had a chance to cool slightly and the juices have settled.

In many recipes I've given an indication of what I consider to be the preferred serving temperature. "Serve immediately" means just that; the dish loses its charm as it cools. On the other hand, I hope you won't get in a hurry and ignore instructions to "let it rest 15 minutes before serving" or "allow it to come to room temperature before serving." For those dishes, a rest period will bring out their best.

You'll also notice that I repeatedly suggest using a warm serving bowl or platter for your finished dish. Warming your serving piece slightly by putting it in a low oven for a couple of minutes helps to keep the food hot. Don't overdo it, however; the serving dish doesn't need to be hot, just warm. Too much heat can crack a dish.

Even when we have guests, I like the informality of serving family style, with food in large bowls or platters that we pass at the table. In your own home, you may be more comfortable with plate service, putting single portions of the meat and side dishes on each plate yourself before serving it.

ABOUT LEFTOVERS

Always store leftovers in airtight containers or with the top of the dish covered securely with plastic wrap. Leftover side dishes can give you a head start on meals the next day. Slowly rewarmed, or just removed from the refrigerator in time to come to room temperature, they can make a quick and satisfying lunch with a slice of bread or a mug of chicken broth. If reheating, take pains not to cook them too much; since the vegetables are already fully cooked, further cooking will cause some loss of texture.

Leftover vegetable dishes can sometimes be stirred into soup or risotto, reheated and served over pasta or rice, or sandwiched between two slices of bread. Just to get you thinking about the possibilities, here are some ideas for using leftovers from the recipes in this book:

Green Beans with Sesame Seeds (page 92)
    Chop and add to stir-fried rice.
Green Beans with Pecorino (page 94)
    Chop, reheat, and toss with pasta.
Buttered Chard with Parmesan (page 68)
    Put in the bottom of a soup bowl with a thick slice of toast;
    add hot chicken broth.
Corn and Limas (page 75)
    Thin with chicken broth to make soup.
Grilled Eggplant Puree, Indian Style (page 86)
    Use as a sandwich spread on a lamb or turkey sandwich.

Baked Ratatouille (page 84)
Serve as a relish for grilled fish.
Eggplant, Tomato, and Chick Pea Stew (page 88)
Reheat and serve with couscous.
Grilled Peppers and Onions (page 103)
Add to a ham, lamb, or tuna sandwich.
Roast Autumn Squash with Cardamom Butter (page 128)
Puree and reheat in a double boiler; or puree, thin with chicken stock, and
reheat to make soup.
Chopped Broccoli with Garlic and Pecorino (page 147)
Reheat and toss with pasta.
Braised Sauerkraut (page 155)
Use on a corned beef sandwich.
Artichoke and Fava Bean Stew (page 40)
Stir into vegetable soup.
Asparagus, Peas, and Scallions (page 43)
Stir into risotto or polenta.
Carrots with Cumin (page 197)
Reheat in chicken broth with grated zucchini, or add to lentil soup.
Wild Mushrooms with Bacon (page 205)
Reheat and toss with pasta.

VEGETABLE COOKING TECHNIQUES AND TIPS

How best to cook what you've brought home from the market? Most vegetables
are suited to several different cooking techniques; if you learn to take advantage of
that fact, you'll find that your repertoire of vegetable dishes is practically unlimited.

If you have always steamed zucchini, consider sauteing or grilling it. If you have
always boiled beets, try baking them. Just by changing techniques, you create a new
dish with new flavors that can revive your own or your family's interest in a particular vegetable.

The following section defines the basic cooking techniques and gives you the
information you need to apply those techniques to specific vegetables.

Baking

Baking means oven-cooking with little or no added liquid. Roasting is the same
process, although traditionally roasting was a word reserved for meat cookery. Today's

menu and recipe writers often use the terms interchangeably, referring to "roasted vegetables" instead of "baked vegetables." Poetic license, I guess. Roasted vegetables sound like they'll be beautifully browned, crusty in parts, and more concentrated in flavor than plain old baked vegetables.

If you are putting a roast in the oven for dinner, you can make it a one-pot meal by surrounding the meat with vegetables that can bake in its juices. If they won't fit in the roasting pan, use a separate baking dish but add some of the drippings from the roast to flavor the vegetables and keep them from drying out. You can bake these alongside your roast:

Carrots—peeled and cut into pieces of desired size
Hard-skinned squash—cut into chunks, peeled, seeds removed
Jerusalem artichokes—scrubbed clean but left whole
Onions—peeled and halved through the root end; the root end should be trimmed but left intact to hold the onion together
Parsnips—peeled and cut into pieces of desired size
Potatoes—peeled only if the skin is coarse; cut into pieces of desired size
Rutabagas—peeled and cut into pieces of desired size
Sweet potatoes—peeled and cut into pieces of desired size
Turnips—peeled and cut into pieces of desired size

The baking dish can be covered or uncovered. Covering the dish creates steam which allows vegetables to cook faster; it also keeps vegetables from drying out before they have cooked through. I bake beets (page 48) and Jerusalem artichokes (page 134) in a covered baking dish. In an uncovered dish, you get more browned, crusty edges and crisp exteriors, but you may have to baste or turn the vegetables occasionally to keep them from drying out. Tomatoes have enough natural moisture to be baked uncovered (page 111); some vegetables, like onions (page 210), can be baked covered to soften them, then uncovered and allowed to brown and caramelize.

Baking small pieces of moist vegetables with breadcrumbs is another popular technique. I've used it to make Tomato Bread Crisp (page 112) and Cauliflower Gratin (page 201). If you try this technique with other vegetables, be sure to cut them into small pieces, to layer them not too thickly in the baking dish with the breadcrumbs, and to add a generous quantity of olive oil or butter for moisture. In general, when baking uncovered, use a low-sided dish or tray to allow for good air circulation.

Sauteing and Stir-Frying

To saute is to cook, uncovered, in a slope-sided skillet in a small amount of fat. *Sauter* means to jump in French; with a flick of the wrist, French chefs make their sauteed vegetables "jump" in the pan to keep them moving and heat them through evenly. Stir-frying is the Chinese equivalent of this technique. Stir-frying is done in a slope-sided wok, with a spatula to keep the contents moving. Chefs who have a one-handled wok may not even use a spatula; like a French chef, they flip the contents of the wok with their wrists.

Sauteing is a dry-heat method; no liquid is added. For that reason, sauteing is best suited to vegetables with a high moisture content like mushrooms, cucumbers, summer squash, and sweet peppers. It's also best to cut vegetables into small pieces for sauteing; large pieces burn before they cook through.

To saute, preheat a thin film of butter, oil, or pork fat in a skillet; when the fat is hot, add the vegetables, then toss or stir as necessary to keep the vegetables moving. Adjust the heat so that the vegetables cook through without burning. If you want to season the vegetables with onion, garlic, ginger, chiles, and/or spices, add these to the fat before the vegetables to give them a chance to release their fragrance. In contrast, many herbs lose a lot of their punch with prolonged heating and should be added to the skillet when the vegetables are almost done.

I also use the saute technique to reheat vegetables that have been previously cooked. That's what most restaurants do—they cook the green beans in the afternoon, then reheat them to order. The technique is a great time-saver when you're having dinner guests. You can boil or steam the vegetables a few hours ahead, then reheat them at the last minute in butter or oil with seasonings.

To preserve the vegetable's color and texture when you boil or steam it ahead, drain it in a sieve or colander and "shock" it under cold running water or in a bowl of ice water to stop the cooking. Drain well, pat dry, then cover and refrigerate until ready to use. Small cauliflower or broccoli pieces, green beans, brussels sprouts, leafy greens, okra, baby artichoke slices or wedges, asparagus, carrots, parsnips, potatoes, rutabagas, and turnips are among the vegetables that can be cooked first, then reheated in a saute pan.

You can easily create new dishes by combining vegetables in a saute or stir-fry, or by pre-cooking vegetables separately and reheating them together in butter or oil. Consider some of these combinations:

Brussels sprouts and turnips
Green beans and halved cherry tomatoes
Sliced okra and halved cherry tomatoes

19

Asparagus and shiitake mushrooms
Diced fennel and diced potatoes
Sweet peppers and corn
Zucchini and corn
Quartered artichoke bottoms and mushrooms
Green beans, fava beans (or frozen limas), and corn
Grated crookneck squash and grated carrots
Broccoli and cauliflower
Peas and turnips
Sliced leeks and sliced potatoes

Broiling

To broil is to cook by direct overhead heat, typically from an oven's built-in gas flame or electric broiler element. A few moments under a preheated broiler can contribute an appetizing browned surface to vegetable dishes. Because they provide such intense heat, broilers aren't often used to cook vegetables from start to finish; they would burn the vegetables before they cooked through. Moist vegetables like eggplant and tomato are exceptions. Well-oiled eggplant slices or tomato halves can be cooked under a broiler, but they should be positioned far enough away from the heat to cook them through without burning. Be sure to preheat your broiler for 5 to 10 minutes before broiling.

Grilling

A charcoal or gas-fired grill provides heat from below, with the food positioned above the heat on a rack. I use charcoal instead of gas because it's what I have, and because I like the smoky, outdoorsy taste the coals provide.

Grilling has gotten a lot of attention in recent years because it's such an easy way to impart flavor without adding much fat. That's as true for vegetables as it is for red meat, poultry, and fish. Carrots halved lengthwise and lightly brushed with olive oil are magnificent on the grill; charcoal grilling caramelizes their natural sugar and intensifies their taste. In *taquerías* (taco shops) in San Francisco's Mission district, the cooks put whole oiled scallions on the grill; they're a wonderful accompaniment for tacos, grilled meat, or fish.

Whenever you're grilling meat, consider a grilled vegetable too. Some vegetables can be placed on the grill raw; others benefit from pre-cooking (blanching) in boiling salted water until they are barely tender, then "finishing" on the grill. Nearly all vegetables (corn and sweet peppers are an exception) should be oiled before grilling, using vegetable or olive oil seasoned to your taste with salt, pepper, herbs, and spices. The following vegetables perform well on a grill:

Asparagus
    Blanch first, pat dry, brush with oil (see page 43).
Carrots
    Halve lengthwise and, brush with oil (see page 194).
Corn
    Peel back husk and remove silk; replace husk and tie the ends with string; soak in cold water 15 minutes, then grill, turning often, until hot throughout, about 15 minutes.
Eggplant
    Slice and brush with oil (see page 87).
Fennel
    Blanch first, pat dry, brush with oil.
Leeks
    Blanch first, pat dry, brush with oil.
Mushrooms
    Brush with oil (see page 206).
Onions
    Halve bulb onions, brush with oil, and cook in a covered grill until tender. Brush thick onion slices with oil and cook directly on the grid (a hinged basket grill, available in well-stocked kitchenware stores, will make it easier to keep the slices together). Brush scallions with oil and cook directly on the grid.
Potatoes
    Boil small new potatoes until just tender, pat dry, brush with oil, skewer whole, and grill; or halve boiled waxy potatoes, brush with oil, and grill.
Summer Squash
    Blanch first or not, as you prefer. If blanched first, brown quickly on a hot grill; if raw, cook more slowly on a cooler part of the grill. Halve zucchini and crookneck squash lengthwise; halve turban-shaped squash horizontally. Brush with oil before grilling.
Sweet Peppers
    Grill whole, turning as needed to blister and blacken the skin all around; transfer to a paper bag and close it to allow the peppers to steam until cool, then peel and scrape away the blackened skin. Do not rinse. Halve peppers and remove seeds and ribs.

21

Tomatoes

Grill whole (cored) or halved until softened; grill thick slices in a hinged basket grill (available in well-stocked kitchenware stores). Skewer cherry tomatoes, brush with oil, and grill.

Vegetable Kebabs

Don't forget that you can thread small pieces or chunks of any of the afore-mentioned vegetables on metal skewers to make colorful kebabs. Be sure the vegetables you combine on a skewer will cook through in about the same time; or put only one type of vegetable on each skewer, then combine them to serve.

Steaming

Cooking in the steam generated by boiling water is a popular and effective way to cook many vegetables. Steaming takes longer than boiling, but it has at least a couple of advantages. For one, boiled vegetables can quickly go from cooked to over-cooked, from crisp to waterlogged; steaming doesn't demand such precise timing. Because they aren't in direct contact with water, steamed vegetables don't easily get soggy. Also, steamed vegetables retain more of the water-soluble vitamins (the B vitamins and vitamin C) and minerals.

Hardware stores, supermarkets, and kitchenware stores carry perforated metal baskets for steaming vegetables. You put the basket in a pot with an inch or so of boiling water (the bottom of the basket should sit above, not in, the water), add your vegetables, cover the pot, and steam until done. A Chinese bamboo steamer—which is what I use—serves the same purpose. However, you can't set a bamboo steamer directly over a conventional pot or skillet because the sides may scorch from the heat of the burner. My steamer came with a wide-rimmed aluminum pot that supports it; otherwise, position the steamer in a wok filled with an inch or so of boiling water.

One disadvantage to steaming is that green vegetables such as broccoli and green beans turn khaki-green in a covered pot. The acid in the vegetable can't escape and it denatures the chlorophyll, the compound responsible for the green color. You can steam green vegetables uncovered but it takes a long time. If you want to retain the bright green color of green vegetables, boil them instead of steaming.

Steaming, like boiling, is a fat-free cooking method. However, it's undeniable that a little olive oil or butter adds taste appeal. You don't need a complicated, ca-loric sauce; just a drizzle of extra-virgin olive oil or a thin pat of unsalted butter tossed with hot steamed vegetables provides satisfaction.

Look at the recipe for Swiss Chard with Anchovy Butter (page 69) for another approach. In that dish, the hot cooked vegetable is tossed with softened flavored butter at the last minute. The butter melts to form a delicious "sauce." That same anchovy butter would be tasty on steamed green beans, broccoli, or cauliflower. Or make another type of flavored butter for seasoning steamed vegetables. Here are some suggested butters for dressing steamed green beans, zucchini, peas, spinach, brussels sprouts, carrots, cauliflower, or broccoli:

Dill Butter
   Soften butter and mix with minced fresh dill, mustard, salt, and pepper.
Garlic Butter
   Pound garlic to a paste with salt, then mix with softened butter and pepper.
Lemon Caper Butter
   Soften butter and mix with grated lemon zest, chopped capers, salt, and pepper.
Maître d'Hôtel Butter
   Soften butter and mix with minced parsley, minced chives, lemon juice, salt, and pepper.
Tarragon Butter
   Soften butter and mixed with minced tarragon, minced shallots or scallions, salt, and pepper.

Boiling

To boil is to cook in direct contact with boiling water. To prevent loss of color and nutrients, boil vegetables as rapidly as possible. My recipes advise boiling in a large quantity of salted water. A large quantity of water will return to a boil quickly after the vegetables are added; salt flavors the water and raises the boiling point slightly so the vegetables cook faster. How much salt? I use about a teaspoon per quart of water, 2 to 3 tablespoons in an 8-quart pot. I use inexpensive table salt for this and reserve coarse kosher salt for seasoning.

After vegetables are boiled, they should be drained thoroughly in a sieve or colander. If they are going to be served right away, I usually put them back in the empty pot, set it over a flame, and shake it until all the water has evaporated. Butter, oil, and seasonings cling better to thoroughly dry vegetables.

If you are cooking vegetables ahead of time and plan to reheat them later (see Sauteing, page 19), you need to cool them quickly to stop the cooking and set the color. When they are done cooking, drain them in a sieve or colander, then either put them immediately in a bowl of ice water or run them under cold running water until they are cool. Drain, pat dry, cover, and refrigerate them until you're ready to use them.

Braising

Cooking in a covered pot with a small amount of added liquid is known as braising. Braising can be done on top of the stove or in the oven. Often when I braise vegetables I cook them through in a flavorful liquid such as chicken stock, tomato sauce, or apple cider, then uncover the pot and allow the liquid to boil down. Typically, you should braise in just enough liquid to keep the vegetables from sticking or burning before they cook through. Choose a pot large enough to hold the vegetables in one layer; they should all be in contact with the liquid.

As an example of braising in chicken stock, see Jerusalem Artichokes and Peas (page 135); Sweet and Sour Leeks (page 53) is an example of braising in tomato sauce.

Deep-Frying

Many cookbooks have recipes for deep-fried vegetables cooked by immersion in hot oil. The vegetables are usually coated with flour or a batter first and served hot from the fryer. They can be delicious, but I avoid that method for a couple of reasons. Foods fried in deep fat absorb a lot of that fat and consequently are high in calories. So are some of my favorite vegetable dishes, like Leeks Baked in Mustard Cream (page 54), Classic Potato Gratin (page 217), or Old-Fashioned Creamed Spinach (page 186), but they have an advantage that fried foods don't have—they don't have to be made at the last minute. With two strikes against them—the calories and the demanding timing—deep-fried vegetables aren't often on the menu at my house.

Microwaving

I am one of a dying breed—a cook without a microwave oven. I don't doubt their capabilities; too many good cooks I know swear by them. It's just that I love all the sensual parts of cooking—the stirring, the smelling, the watching. I enjoy that feeling of anticipation as my appetite grows and good smells start to come from the pots. My husband and I open a bottle of wine while we prepare and wait for dinner, and we talk over the events of the day. A microwave oven would only speed up the process and rob me of time in the kitchen that I actually relish.

That's why you won't find microwave directions in this book. However, I encourage you to adapt these recipes for use in your microwave if you're so inclined.

WHAT YOU SHOULD KNOW FOR BEST RESULTS

About Salt

I use coarse kosher salt in cooking because I like its mild, clean taste. Try it side by side with table salt and you will notice the difference. Table salt tastes harsh and unpleasantly salty.

Because tolerance for salt varies, I have specified "salt to taste" in most recipes. Where you may not want to taste the mixture—a batter containing raw eggs, for example—I have specified the quantity of salt that appeals to my palate.

I prefer to salt vegetables at the start of cooking and then to add a little more at the end if necessary. When you add salt at the beginning, it knits itself into the dish. By the end of the cooking, you don't perceive the salt, you just taste that the dish is well seasoned.

About Chicken Stock

If you can find the time and freezer space to make homemade chicken stock regularly, you're more organized than I am. For convenience, I use canned chicken stock in many vegetable dishes. However, even the brand I like is too salty for my taste, so I water it down to an acceptable salt level before using it. Bouillon cubes and powdered soup bases are, to my palate, a much less desirable option.

About Vinaigrette

A vinaigrette is a dressing made by mixing approximately one part wine vinegar with three parts oil. The vinegar can be sherry vinegar, Champagne vinegar, or a high-quality red or white wine vinegar. If you wish, you can substitute lemon juice for the vinegar. Lemon is appealing with carrots, beets, broccoli, spinach, green beans, peppers, and fennel. I almost always use olive oil in vinaigrettes, although occasionally I add a little bit of walnut or hazelnut oil if their nutty flavor would complement the dish. Combine the vinegar and oil in a small bowl with salt and freshly ground black pepper to taste. Whisk; taste and add more oil or vinegar if desired.

About Equipment

Well-made kitchen equipment is a pleasure to use and can truly give you better results. You won't believe how much faster and more neatly you can chop an onion with a *sharp* knife. You don't need a kitchen full of specialty peelers and scrapers and expensive pans to make the recipes in this book, but I do find myself using a few modest pieces of equipment again and again. If you don't have them, you may want to acquire them. They'll make cooking easier—and, therefore, more fun.

All of these items can be purchased at well-stocked housewares stores or at restaurant supply stores. The latter tend to have sturdy, high-quality materials built to endure the daily pounding of restaurant use.

CHEESE GRATERS, four-sided and two-sided: I use a four-sided grater to grate Gruyère, Parmesan, cheddar, and other cheeses for recipes. A two-sided grater with a single grating surface and a handle is useful for those dishes that need to have cheese grated directly onto the top of the hot dish.

FOOD MILL: With the advent of the food processor, the food mill has been relegated to the back of many kitchen cabinets. I still use mine, however, to puree potatoes (a food processor turns potatoes into library paste) and other starchy or fibrous vegetables like sweet potatoes and rutabagas.

GRATIN DISH: *Gratin* is the French word for food that has a top crust—such as a breadcrumb or melted cheese crust. To aid in crust formation, these recipes are typically baked in a "gratin dish"—a shallow ovenproof earthenware dish that is usually oval but may be any shape. When my recipes call for a gratin dish, I specify the size of the dish I used. You should try to use a dish of comparable height and volume so that the baking time indicated in the recipe works for you.

HEAVY BAKING SHEET: If you have ever made the same cookie recipe on a thin, flimsy baking sheet and on a heavy baking sheet, I'm sure you've noticed the difference. A thick aluminum sheet—what the restaurant supply stores call a half sheet pan— is a great investment, not only for baking cookies, but also for baking vegetables like the potato "fries" on page 216.

LARGE HEAVY SKILLET, with tight-fitting lid: A 10-inch or 12-inch heavy-bottomed skillet with a tight-fitting lid is essential to getting good results with some of the recipes in this book, such as Braised Turnips (page 189); Eggplant, Tomato, and Chick Pea Stew (page 88); and Braised Fennel with Parmesan (page 168).

LARGE STAINLESS STEEL WIRE-MESH SIEVE: This is useful for draining vegetables after boiling or steaming, especially small batches.

MORTAR AND PESTLE: The mortar is the bowl; the pestle is the grinding implement. I use a white porcelain mortar and pestle to grind whole spices; fresh peppercorns ground in a mortar are even more aromatic than peppercorns ground in a hand-held mill. I also use it to grind garlic and salt to a paste for seasoning mayonnaise or other cold sauces. If you know a research scientist, he or she can probably get you a good mortar and pestle at little cost; they are standard lab equipment. (That's how I got mine.)

PEPPER MILL: Storebought ground pepper is hardly worth using. I use, and I recommend that you use, whole peppercorns ground fresh in a pepper mill. It makes a difference. Occasionally, when I want a very pungent pepper taste, I grind the peppercorns in a mortar with a pestle (see above).

STAINLESS STEEL COLANDER: A colander is very useful for draining vegetables after boiling or steaming.

Keep These on Hand

Good vegetable cooking is simple cooking that doesn't require a lot of ingredients. Still, there are a few items that I consider part of my kitchen's foundation—ingredients that I always want to have in the pantry, in the refrigerator, or close at hand. They are essential to improvisational side-dish cooking at my house. With these few items on hand, I know that I can make something tasty out of whatever the market provides.

ANCHOVIES, canned or bottled: These tiny preserved fish add a pungent, fishy, salty flavor characteristic of many Mediterranean dishes. I love them and use them frequently with broccoli, cauliflower, artichokes, zucchini, tomatoes, sweet peppers, and other vegetables common in Mediterranean countries. They can be minced fine or pounded to a paste and added to butter or olive oil as a flavoring (see Swiss Chard with Anchovy Butter, page 69). Or make a tomato sauce flavored with minced anchovy and garlic for braising cauliflower or sliced sweet peppers. I find that anchovies quickly develop a rancid taste after the bottle or can is opened. I put the extras in a ceramic bowl, cover them completely with olive oil, cover the bowl with plastic wrap, and refrigerate them. If I'm not going to use them within a week or so, I cover them with olive oil and freeze them.

CANNED CHICKEN STOCK: It's not as good as homemade but less trouble (see About Chicken Stock, page 25). I use it, usually watered down to an acceptable salt

level, as a braising medium for many vegetables. As the dish cooks, the stock mingles with the vegetable juices and reduces to a delicious spoonful of sauce or a light glaze. Sometimes I use chicken stock to add a meaty dimension to a tomato sauce (see Artichokes with Saffron, Tomatoes, and Peas, page 38) or a cream sauce (see Baked Leeks in Mustard Cream, page 54).

CANNED TOMATOES: When fresh tomatoes aren't in season, canned tomatoes are an acceptable substitute for sauces and braised dishes. I use canned plum tomatoes imported from Italy. If I don't use the whole can, I transfer the remaining tomatoes to a plastic container, refrigerate them, and try to use them within a week. I don't usually chop the canned tomatoes before adding them to a dish. Instead, I gently squeeze them through my fingers directly into the pot, taking care not to splatter juice everywhere.

CAPERS: The caper bush is native to the Mediterranean. Its flower buds are pickled in brine and sold in supermarkets and Mediterranean markets. I like their piquant, vinegary flavor with broccoli, cauliflower, carrots, tomatoes, green beans, eggplant, sweet peppers, zucchini, beets, leeks, and onions. I prefer small capers to large ones; if I find myself with a jar of large capers, I usually chop them coarsely before using. Some people rinse capers, but I like the briny taste; if you don't, rinse and pat them dry before using. They will keep in their brine in the refrigerator for months.

FRESH HERBS: I wouldn't be without the fresh herbs in my garden; they add fragrance to many vegetable dishes. I regularly grow rosemary, oregano, thyme, sage, tarragon, and chives, and value these ornamental perennials as much for their beauty as for the contribution they make to my cooking. I also occasionally grow annuals— basil, parsley, dill, chervil—and encourage you to grow them if you can't find them readily at the grocery store. They perform beautifully in pots, and it's such a treat to be able to run outside and harvest them as needed. Mint is so invasive that I don't have it in my garden, but it's readily available in supermarkets and useful with many vegetables.

    After washing and drying fresh herbs, separate the leaves from the tough stems, if any. Chop the leaves shortly before using them to get the biggest punch. Some herbs—generally the more pungent ones like rosemary, sage, oregano, and thyme— benefit from being added at the beginning of the cooking process. The more delicate herbs—parsley, dill, chervil, chives—lose some of their fresh liveliness when heated, so I add them at the end of the cooking process, often tossing them with the hot vegetable just before serving.

Fresh herbs are not good keepers. Put large bunches in a glass with the stems in a couple of inches of water; cover with a plastic bag and refrigerate. If you have only a few stems, refrigerate them wrapped in paper towels and overwrapped in plastic; they will keep for a few days.

GARLIC: A little minced fresh garlic, its fragrance released by warming in olive oil or butter, enhances almost any vegetable dish. The only vegetables that I don't regularly season with garlic are the supersweet ones—sweet potatoes, corn, parsnips, winter squash—although that isn't a hard and fast rule (I put garlic in Creamed Corn and Hominy, page 76).

Garlic quickly burns if it is cooked in too hot a pan. I usually add it to the olive oil or butter over moderately low heat, sauteing until the fragrance is released.

Garlic should be kept in a cool, dark, dry place. I keep mine in a "garlic cellar," a lidded jar with holes in the side for air circulation. Once you have broken the bulb's papery outer skin, it starts to dry out and deteriorate. I try to break off one clove at a time, leaving the bulb as intact as possible to preserve its moisture.

To peel garlic cloves, I smash them lightly with the side of a large knife, slip off the skin, then cut off the brown tip. If there is any sign that the clove is sprouting, I cut it in half lengthwise and lift out any trace of green sprout, which has a strong taste. If the cloves seem dry or have a strong odor instead of a sweetly pleasant one, I don't use them. I usually mince garlic by hand with a knife, although sometimes I pound it in a mortar if I want a paste consistency (see Swiss Chard with Anchovy Butter, page 69). Pounding it, like pressing it with a garlic press, releases stronger flavors.

OLIVE OIL, two kinds: I use a light, inexpensive olive oil for cooking, but I also keep a much more flavorful extra virgin olive oil on hand for seasoning boiled or steamed vegetables. These expensive, fruity oils lose much of their flavor when heated. Save them to drizzle on steamed green beans, broccoli, cauliflower, asparagus, Swiss chard, or spinach after cooking.

PARMESAN CHEESE: The word is a shortened Anglicized version of Parmigiano-Reggiano, the only type of "Parmesan" I use. Authentic Parmigiano-Reggiano comes from a designated region in Italy and you can tell it's authentic because the name is stenciled on the rind. I buy it about a pound at a time and grate it as I need it for best flavor. Domestic "Parmesan" bears little resemblance to the imported product and I don't recommend it. Store Parmesan well wrapped in the refrigerator; it will keep for months.

UNSALTED BUTTER: You can use salted butter in any of these recipes without problem, but I prefer the fresh, clean taste of unsalted butter. It spoils quickly, however, because it lacks the preservative quality of salt. Keep it in the freezer and thaw only as much as you can use in three or four days. After thawing, keep it refrigerated. Taste the butter before using it; if it tastes at all rancid, don't use it—it can spoil the taste of a dish.

About Recipes

A recipe can be a formula, or a recipe can be merely a guide. Recipes for baked goods, for example, are usually written like formulas because the correct proportions are critical to success. For good reason, cake recipes tell you exactly how much flour, how much sugar, and how much fat to use; variations from the recipe can make a major difference in the texture and taste.

Outside of the realm of baking, recipes can be a little less dogmatic, a little more relaxed. Still, the tendency today is away from "a handful of this" recipe writing in favor of recipes that tell you exactly how much to use, in exactly what pots, at exactly what temperature, for exactly how long. The aim, of course, is to improve your chances of duplicating the author's results.

At some point, however, success with a recipe depends on your own good judgment. No matter how specific a recipe writer tries to be, there are variables the writer can't know. How juicy are your tomatoes? What shape is your eggplant? What shape is your dish? How accurate is your oven? Are you cooking on a powerful professional range or on a standard home range? All of these variables can affect timing, proportions, and results.

Every recipe in this book has been rigorously tested in a home kitchen. They do work. But occasionally you must exercise your own judgment. If the recipe says to cook it 20 minutes but your dish looks done after 15, turn the heat off! I have tried to give various indications of when something is done so you don't have to depend on the clock; it's done when it's done, not when the clock says it is.

Recipes can give you ideas, broaden your repertoire, teach you techniques and short cuts, and provide the information you need for successful results, but they are not meant to be slavishly followed if your nose, your eyes, and your experience tell you otherwise. Don't surrender your good judgment to a recipe; if your taste buds tell you to cook it longer, add more vinegar, or lower the heat, do it.

SPRING

ARTICHOKES	*Artichokes with Saffron, Tomatoes, and Peas*
	Artichoke and Fava Bean Stew
ASPARAGUS	*Grilled Asparagus with Olive Oil and Lemon*
	Asparagus, Peas, and Scallions
BEETS	*Shredded Beets and Red Cabbage*
	Baked Beets with Butter, Parsley, and Dill
FAVA BEANS	*Couscous with Fava Beans*
LEEKS	*Sweet and Sour Leeks*
	Baked Leeks in Mustard Cream
PEAS	*Peas and Pods with Tarragon*
	Peas in Crème Fraîche

SPRING MAKES its presence known at the produce market with a great rush of green—artichokes, asparagus, fava beans, pale leeks, English peas, sugar snap peas, snow peas. That fresh "green" taste is so welcome after months of root vegetables that I like to cook the first spring vegetables as simply as possible: steamed and buttered English peas mixed with a little *crème fraîche* (page 61); blanched asparagus rolled in olive oil and grilled (page 43); snow peas quickly stir-fried with peanut oil and salt.

But spring vegetables are also suited to more imaginative preparations. Simple stews made by braising two or three spring vegetables together can be particularly satisfying. Consider artichokes with fava beans, for example, or asparagus with peas and scallions. Yet even these slightly more complex combinations have a delicacy about them that distinguishes them from the more robust flavors I favor at other times of year.

ARTICHOKES

Most of the country's artichokes are grown in coastal northern California, where they get the cool, foggy weather they like. Living less than two hours from Castroville, the "artichoke capital of the world," I can find high quality, reasonably priced artichokes in the market much of the year, although quality and supply peak in the spring. I'm aware that others are not so lucky, that firm, fresh-picked artichokes are a rare and expensive treat in some parts of the country. Even in California, where artichokes are commonplace, many cooks don't get enough mileage out of them. They know how to steam them whole and serve them as a first course with a dipping sauce, but they don't realize that both the walnut-sized "babies" and the larger globes make delicious side dishes.

If you have had only frozen, canned, or bottled artichokes, I urge you to buy some fresh ones when you can find them in decent shape at an affordable price. Frozen and canned artichokes tend to taste washed out and watery; bottled marinated artichoke hearts taste more like the marinade than like artichokes. When you try them fresh, you can appreciate their nutty, slightly bitter, green bean-like taste.

Artichokes do have one drawback at the dinner table. Some component of the vegetable—possibly an organic acid called cynarin, unique to artichokes—makes most wines taste unpleasant. Have a sip of wine, a taste of artichoke, and another sip of wine to experience this phenomenon. If the artichoke is combined with other vegetables or cooked with fat and spices, the effect is muted, but I still don't serve artichokes when I'm serving an important wine.

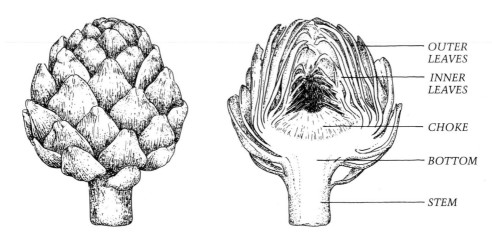

OUTER LEAVES

INNER LEAVES

CHOKE

BOTTOM

STEM

Anatomy of an Artichoke

The outermost artichoke leaves are dark green, somewhat tough, and have a thorny tip (except on the babies and some new, large "thornless" varieties that have rounded tips). All the leaves are attached to the artichoke at its thick, meaty base—the artichoke bottom. You can pull the leaves back and break them off at the base. The leaves get paler and more tender as you move toward the center of the artichoke. The innermost leaves are very tender, with prickly purple tips. Underneath them is the "choke" itself—an inedible collection of tiny prickly leaves and fuzzy hairs attached to the artichoke bottom. Baby artichokes—the size of a jumbo egg or smaller—usually have neither a choke nor the prickly-tipped center leaves. Apart from their tough green outer leaves, they are entirely edible.

Artichoke terminology is confusing. Artichoke "heart" can mean two things. An artichoke heart can be a baby artichoke trimmed of its tough outer leaves, its tip, and stem. Frozen artichoke hearts and marinated artichoke hearts in jars are made with these trimmed babies. An artichoke heart can also be a large artichoke trimmed down to its pale green, tender leaves, with the choke and prickly innermost leaves removed.

TO SELECT

Artichokes range in size from about 2 ounces to 20 ounces. All are fully mature when picked; the small ones are found down among the plant fronds where they receive less sun. Size is no indication of quality, so buy the size that's best suited to your recipe. Large artichokes have the meaty bottoms required for some recipes; other recipes work best with the tender, choke-free baby artichokes.

Whatever their size, artichokes should be firm and compact. The artichoke is a flower bud; if it has started to open it is too old. Avoid any that feel spongy when squeezed. Frost will darken the outer leaves of an artichoke but it doesn't harm the flavor; in fact, some say it improves it.

TO STORE

Refrigerate artichokes in a perforated plastic bag in the vegetable crisper and use within 2 to 3 days.

COOKING TIPS

Trimming When trimming artichokes, rub each newly cut part with lemon to prevent browning.

Artichokes with Saffron, Tomatoes, and Peas (page 38)

ARTICHOKES WITH SAFFRON, TOMATOES, AND PEAS

This beautiful stew uses only the hearts of large artichokes. But don't throw out the leaves! Save them and steam them the next day over boiling salted water, then serve them as a first course with homemade mayonnaise or the Yogurt Scallion Sauce on page 87.

Instead of saffron, you could season this dish with chopped fresh tarragon or mint. Serve it with roast lamb, swordfish steaks, breaded veal scallops, grilled tuna with lemon, or baked chicken thighs.

Serves 4

> 1 lemon
> 2 medium artichokes
> 2 tablespoons olive oil
> ¾ cup minced scallions (green onions)
> 2 cloves garlic, minced
> 1 cup chopped fresh tomatoes or canned tomatoes, with juice
> ¾ cup chicken stock
> ⅛ teaspoon saffron threads
> Salt and freshly ground black pepper
> 1 cup fresh or frozen peas
> Parmesan cheese

1. Fill a medium bowl with cold water and add the juice of half the lemon. Cut off and discard all but ¾ inch of each artichoke stem. Rub the cut ends with the remaining half lemon. One by one, pull back the artichoke leaves (be careful of the prickly tips) until they break off naturally; remove the leaves until you reach the tender, pale green "heart." With a serrated knife, cut off about the top ¾ inch of the artichokes.

2. Cut the artichokes in half from tip to stem. With a spoon, scrape out all the prickly hairs and the soft inner leaves that have sharp tips. Rub the cut parts with lemon as you go to prevent browning. Turn the artichoke halves over and, with a small, sharp knife, trim away any dark green outer parts, including the tough, dark green layer on the stem. Rub with lemon. Cut each artichoke half in half again from tip to stem and place the quarters in the bowl of acidulated water.

3. Heat the olive oil in a heavy 10-inch skillet over moderate heat. Add the green onions and saute 5 minutes. Add the garlic and saute until fragrant, about 1 minute.

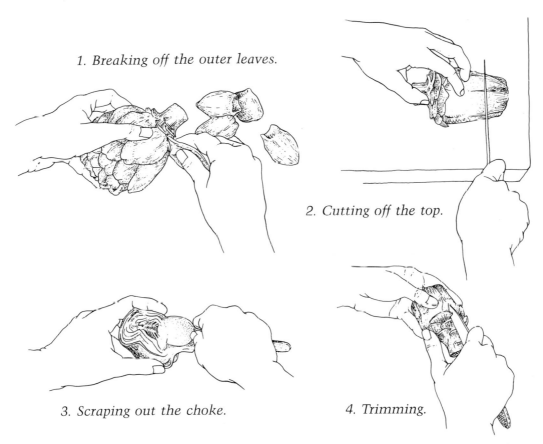

1. Breaking off the outer leaves.

2. Cutting off the top.

3. Scraping out the choke.

4. Trimming.

Add the tomatoes. (If using canned tomatoes, carefully squeeze them between your fingers to break them up, or chop them coarsely.) Add the chicken stock and saffron. Bring the mixture to a simmer, lower the heat, and continue simmering until the tomato sauce is reduced and quite thick, about 15 minutes.

4. Remove the artichokes from the water and add them to the skillet, one cut side down. Spoon a little of the sauce over them. Season with salt and pepper, then cover the skillet and cook until the artichokes are tender, about 20 minutes. If using fresh peas, add them about 10 minutes before the artichokes are done; if using frozen peas, add them about 3 minutes before the artichokes are done. Taste and adjust the seasoning. Serve each person 2 artichoke wedges; spoon the peas and tomato sauce over the artichokes. Sprinkle liberally with freshly grated Parmesan cheese.

ARTICHOKE AND FAVA BEAN STEW

In Italy, these two vegetables are often braised together because they're in season at the same time. Sicilian cooks add peas, replace the thyme with fresh mint, and call the dish *la frittedda*. This accommodating stew could accompany baked salmon, grilled squid or shrimp, roast chicken, pork, or lamb.

Serves 4

> 1 lemon
> 10 baby artichokes, about the size of large walnuts
> 2 pounds fresh fava beans
> 2 tablespoons olive oil
> ⅓ cup minced scallions (green onions)
> Salt and freshly ground black pepper
> 2 sprigs fresh thyme

1. Fill a medium bowl with cold water; add the juice of half the lemon. Peel back the outer leaves on each artichoke until they break off at the base. Keep removing leaves until you reach the pale green "heart." Cut about ⅓ inch off the top of the heart to remove the pointed tips; cut away any stem. Trim the base to remove any dark green parts. Immediately rub each trimmed heart all over with the remaining half lemon and drop the hearts into the acidulated water.

2. Remove the fava beans from the pods. To peel the individual beans, blanch them in boiling water for 30 seconds, then drain. While they are hot, pinch open the end that was not connected to the pod. The peeled bean will slip out easily.

3. Heat the olive oil in a heavy 12-inch skillet over moderate heat. Add the scallions and saute until they soften slightly, about 2 minutes. Remove the artichokes from the water and cut them in half. Immediately add them to the skillet and toss to coat them with oil. Season generously with salt and pepper. Add the thyme sprigs and 2 tablespoons of water. Cover, reduce the heat to low, and cook until the artichokes are tender, about 30 minutes. Check occasionally; add a little more water if necessary to keep the artichokes from sticking.

4. Add the fava beans and 2 tablespoons of water. Cover and cook until the beans are just tender, about 6 to 8 minutes. Do not overcook or they will lose their bright green color. Season the stew to taste with more salt and pepper; remove the thyme sprigs. The dish benefits from resting 5 to 10 minutes before serving.

OTHER SERVING SUGGESTIONS

BRAISED ARTICHOKE BOTTOMS WITH PANCETTA AND THYME Cut artichoke bottoms into wedges and braise them with pancetta, thyme, and enough water or stock to keep them from sticking. Toss in some cut-up boiled or roasted potatoes at the end, if you like.

ARTICHOKES AND MORELS IN CREAM If you are lucky enough to find wild morel mushrooms—or can afford the storebought ones—try braising them in cream and stock with shallots and some wedges of artichoke bottom.

ARTICHOKE BOTTOMS WITH CREAMED SPINACH OR PEAS Fill whole boiled artichoke bottoms with creamed spinach or peas in cream.

VEGETABLE STEW Trim baby artichokes as described in step 1 of Artichoke and Fava Bean Stew, page 40. Cut them into halves, quarters, or thin slices through the base. Braise them in butter or oil with other spring vegetables of your choice (peas, leeks, whole shallots, sugar snap peas, fava beans, asparagus, scallions, or carrots) and just enough stock or water to keep the stew from sticking.

ASPARAGUS

To me, asparagus and spring are as closely connected as turkey and Thanksgiving. The arrival of the bright green bundled spears in the market in early March is the first sign that our rainy northern California winter is almost behind us. Even their fresh, grassy flavor suggests spring to me, so strongly that I don't want asparagus at any other time of year. I like asparagus so much that I usually serve them as a separate (first) course, but the same preparations work as main dish components, too.

TO SELECT

Look for firm spears with good green color and a tightly closed tip. Avoid any that feel limp or woody and any with tips that are starting to open.

Thick spears or thin? It depends on your taste; if in good condition, they'll be tender either way. Just be sure to buy spears of approximately the same size so that they cook in the same amount of time.

The tip of an asparagus spear is its most tender part. If you want to offer guests the *crème de la crème* of asparagus, serve the tips (about the first 4 inches) and save the rest of the spears for soup.

You may occasionally see fresh white asparagus in specialty produce markets, usually priced at a premium. They are not a separate variety; they are normal asparagus grown under mulch to protect them from the sun. I don't think they're worth the price difference, but you should try them if you're curious.

TO STORE   Refrigerate asparagus in the vegetable crisper in a perforated plastic bag and use them as soon as possible. If you need to keep them for more than a day, wrap the butt ends in damp paper towels.

COOKING TIPS   ***Trimming***   Wash and drain the spears. Hold a spear with one hand at about the middle and the other near the bottom end. Bend it gently. It will break naturally at the point at which the spear becomes tough. Discard the tough end. Thin spears don't need peeling and, in my opinion, thick spears rarely do if you have snapped them properly. However, if the green skin looks coarse or thick, you can peel it with a vegetable peeler down to the pale "heart." Peeled spears will cook more quickly.

Cooking   Some people cook asparagus upright in a special deep steamer with a cover. The butt ends cook in the water and the tips cook in the steam. I don't have one of those pots and don't recommend cooking asparagus covered; they quickly lose their bright green color.

I find that asparagus cook evenly if boiled, uncovered, in a large quantity of salted water. Timing depends on size, and you have to pay attention to get it right. The spears quickly go from perfectly crisp-tender to mushy. When they get close to done, start pulling spears out with tongs and testing them. Remember that they will continue to cook as they cool unless you shock them in cold water. Drain and pat them dry before dressing them.

GRILLED ASPARAGUS WITH OLIVE OIL AND LEMON

My husband Doug and I first had grilled asparagus in a tapas bar in Valencia, Spain. It's now our favorite way to prepare them. The important thing is to blanch the spears just until they are starting to get tender—no longer; they will continue to cook on the grill. It's also important to have a hot fire.

Serves 4

> **2 pounds asparagus**
> **1 tablespoon extra virgin olive oil**
> **Kosher salt**
> **Lemon wedges**

1. Wash and trim the asparagus (see page 42). Bring a large pot of salted water to a boil over high heat. Add the asparagus spears and boil until they just lose their rawness; cooking time will vary according to thickness, but medium-thick spears will take about 3 minutes. Drain and shock them under cold running water to stop the cooking. Drain again and pat them completely dry in kitchen towels.

2. Prepare a hot charcoal fire. On a platter, toss the asparagus spears with the olive oil until evenly coated. Place them on the grate above the coals, being sure to place them across the bars so they don't fall in. Watch carefully; they can burn quickly. When they are lightly browned on one side, roll them over with tongs to brown the other. Total cooking time is about 3 minutes. Transfer the asparagus to a serving platter; sprinkle them with salt. Garnish with lemon.

ASPARAGUS, PEAS, AND SCALLIONS

Ready in 10 minutes, this spring vegetable stew is a good dish for beginning cooks. The only way to ruin it is to overcook the asparagus—which you won't do. Otherwise, it's straightforward and easy and it can be a launching point for variations: substitute diced potatoes for the asparagus, or stir in some sauteed mushrooms at the end, or use lima beans in place of peas.

Use either thick asparagus or thin—whichever looks best in the market—but adjust the cooking times accordingly. Medium to thick asparagus will cook in about the same time as small fresh peas. If your asparagus tips are skinny, start the peas first.

Serves 4

> 1½ tablespoons unsalted butter
> 12 ounces asparagus tips (in 1-inch lengths)
> 1 cup fresh peas or frozen petite peas
> ½ cup chicken stock
> ¼ cup finely minced scallions (green onions)
> ¾ teaspoon minced fresh tarragon
> 1 ounce prosciutto, finely minced
> Freshly ground black pepper

1. Melt the butter in a large skillet over moderate heat. Add the asparagus tips and fresh peas, if using. Stir to coat the vegetables with butter. Add the chicken stock, bring it to a simmer, and cover the pan. Cook until the asparagus tips and peas are almost done. Timing will depend on the thickness of the tips and the size and age of the peas, but 5 minutes should be about right. If using frozen peas, add them a couple of minutes before the asparagus tips are done; they need to just heat through.

2. When the vegetables are almost done, uncover the pan, raise the heat, and allow the excess liquid to evaporate. Stir in the scallions, tarragon, and prosciutto. Season to taste with pepper. If the chicken stock was salted, the dish will probably not need salt, but taste it before serving.

OTHER SERVING SUGGESTIONS

SIMPLY ASPARAGUS With asparagus, simple ideas are best. A neat bundle of boiled spears rolled in butter or olive oil and lightly salted needs no other adornment. For a change of pace, season buttered asparagus spears with minced dill or garnish them with some finely chopped hard-cooked egg or grated Parmesan.

STIR-FRIED ASPARAGUS Cut the raw spears into any desired lengths and stir-fry them in a wok in corn or peanut oil. Add water or chicken stock a little at a time, using just enough to steam the spears. Some thin-sliced shiitake mushrooms, either fresh or reconstituted dried ones, can be stir-fried along with the asparagus.

ASPARAGUS IN VEGETABLE STEWS Asparagus spears cut into bite-size lengths can also play a role in vegetable stews, as in Asparagus, Peas, and Scallions (page 43). Try them with lima beans, fava beans, scallions, and/or mushrooms.

BEETS

Grow your own beets and pull them up when they are no bigger than a ping pong ball if you want to taste a vegetable as sweet as candy. You get a dividend, too: the fresh, vitamin-packed, blemish-free greens, which almost always look limp and battered by the time they get to the supermarket.

Even supermarket beets, if they're not too big, old, and woody, have a notably high sugar content. Food writer Harold McGee reports that beets can be as much as 8 percent sugar, very high for a vegetable. Small wonder that scientists looked to beets as a source of commercial sugar.

Because of this unrestrained sweetness, beets don't go with everything. I don't think they flatter fish, for example, but I do think they're delicious with rich meats such as pork roasts and chops, beef brisket, duck, and ham.

Beets can be boiled or baked. I find that boiling drains a lot of the color and flavor out of them. My vote goes to baking, which seems to concentrate the flavor and almost caramelize the sugars.

Red beets stain everything they come into contact with, which is why I prefer to cook them by themselves or with a vegetable that's already red (see Shredded Beets and Red Cabbage, page 46). Some specialty markets also sell golden beets now. Cook them just as you would red beets (although they wouldn't be pretty in the aforementioned cabbage recipe).

TO SELECT
: Beets should feel firm, not spongy. If the tops are attached, they should be fresh and lively looking. Choose small beets over large ones; large ones can be woody.

TO STORE
: If the greens are still attached, remove them and refrigerate them in a perforated plastic bag; use them within a day or two. The beet roots will keep in a plastic bag in the refrigerator for a couple of weeks.

COOKING TIPS
: **Baking** Put washed and dried beets in a baking dish; add a little olive oil and turn to coat the beets lightly with oil. Cover and bake in a 375° oven until tender (test with a small knife). When cool enough to handle, peel. Serve small beets whole; cut larger beets into slices or chunks after baking.

Boiling   Boil unpeeled beets in a large quantity of salted water until tender. If you peel them, pierce the skin, or remove the root end before cooking, they will lose color to the cooking water. Test for doneness with a small sharp knife but do so as few times as possible to minimize color loss. Peel after cooking, as soon as they are cool enough to handle. They get harder to peel as they cool.

SHREDDED BEETS AND RED CABBAGE

I'd never thought of grating raw beets until a caterer friend, Sharon Thomas, suggested it. The food processor does it in seconds and the beets cook quickly. I like them even better paired with shredded red cabbage. Sprinkled with a little balsamic vinegar and slowly braised, the two mingle and blend so well that you almost can't tell what's what. The recipe suggests one way to season the dish—with minced scallions and parsley—but you might try it another time with any of the following: a little garlic, some chopped fresh coriander (cilantro), some grated orange or lemon zest, a bay leaf, a couple of cloves, a pinch of cardamom, or whatever appeals to you.

I would serve this dish with roast chicken or duck, pork, squab, or rabbit.

Serves 4

> ¾ **pound red cabbage**
> 3 **medium beets (about ¾ pound total)**
> 2 **tablespoons butter**
> ¼ **cup balsamic vinegar**
> **Salt and freshly ground black pepper**
> ¼ **cup finely minced scallions (green onions)**
> 2 **tablespoons minced parsley**

Cut the cabbage into wedges; core the wedges and grate them in a food processor fitted with a coarse grating blade. Transfer the cabbage to a 4-quart saucepan. Peel the beets, cut them into wedges, and grate them in the food processor. Transfer them to the pot with the cabbage. Add the butter and 2 tablespoons of the vinegar; season with salt and pepper. Cover and cook over moderate heat, stirring occasionally, until the beets and cabbage are cooked through, about 20 to 25 minutes. Add the scallions, parsley, and remaining 2 tablespoons of vinegar and toss to blend. Taste and adjust the seasoning.

46

BAKED BEETS WITH BUTTER, PARSLEY, AND DILL

The natural sweetness of beets is appealing with fresh pork or ham, turkey, duck, or quail. A braised beef tongue or brisket would be another harmonious choice.

Try to buy beets of the same size so they cook in about the same time. Any size is fine, but those larger than the ones called for in the recipe will take longer to cook.

Serves 4

> 12 small beets, about 1½ inches in diameter
> 1 tablespoon olive oil
> 1½ tablespoons butter
> ¼ cup finely minced scallions (green onions)
> Salt
> 2 tablespoons minced fresh dill
> 1 tablespoon minced parsley
> Red or white wine vinegar (optional)

1. Preheat the oven to 375°. Cut away the beet greens (reserve them for another dish), leaving about ½ inch attached. Wash the beets well and pat them dry. Place them in a lidded baking dish. Add the olive oil and toss to coat the beets with oil. Cover and bake until tender, about 1 hour. (A small knife should slip in and out easily.)

2. Allow the beets to cool for a few minutes, then spear each beet with a fork and peel it with a small knife. Cut small beets in half, larger beets in quarters or even smaller pieces.

3. When ready to serve, melt the butter in a large skillet. Add the scallions and saute until they soften, about 3 minutes. Add the beets and toss to coat them with butter; heat them through. Season with salt. Add the dill and parsley and toss. Remove from the heat and taste; if desired, sprinkle with vinegar. Transfer the beets to a warm bowl and serve immediately.

OTHER SERVING SUGGESTIONS

BEETS WITH BEET GREENS Dress hot cooked beets with butter or olive oil and serve them alongside their cooked greens or sliced and tossed with them.

SEASONINGS FOR BEETS Lemon and orange are compatible flavors, as are spices and flavors commonly used in Indian cooking, such as ginger, turmeric, garlic, mustard seed, coriander, cloves, and cumin.

FAVA BEANS

Mediterranean cooks prize fava beans for their sweet "beany" flavor and creamy texture. I love shelling beans of all kinds, but these are perhaps my favorite. Available in specialty produce markets or in markets catering to an Italian clientele (in some markets they are called broad beans), fava beans look something like limas but are more delicate in flavor and less starchy. The flat beans come encased in a large green pod; string the pod and you'll find a neat line of favas nestled in a fuzzy bed.

TO SELECT
: The bean pods should have a soft velvety feel and should not be overly large or blemished. The big bulging pods are over-mature.

TO STORE
: Refrigerate fava beans in a perforated plastic bag in the vegetable crisper. Use within a couple of days.

COOKING TIPS
: ***Peeling***   String the pod and remove the beans. Fava beans have a thick, bitter skin that should be removed. The easiest way to do that is to bring a pot of water to a boil, add the beans, cook them 30 seconds, then drain. While they are hot, pinch open the end of the bean opposite the end that connected it to the pod. The peeled bean will slip out easily. This can be tedious work by yourself; plan to cook fava beans when you have help in the kitchen. A glass of wine and some conversation make the task much less tiresome.

COUSCOUS WITH FAVA BEANS

This combination of soft green favas with fluffy golden couscous grains is one of my favorites. It well repays the few minutes it takes to peel the beans. Aim for the fava beans and the couscous to be done at the same time so you can combine them and serve them while both are hot; couscous cools off quickly. Serve with braised lamb shanks, lamb stew, or roast leg of lamb with pan juices.

Serves 4

> 2 pounds fava beans (see Note)
> 3 tablespoons unsalted butter
> 4 scallions (green onions), minced
> Salt and freshly ground black pepper
> 1 cup hot chicken stock
> 1 cup couscous (see Note)
> 2 teaspoons minced fresh dill (optional)

1. Remove the fava beans from their pods. To peel the individual beans, blanch them in boiling water for 30 seconds; drain. While they are hot, pinch open the end of the bean opposite the end that connected it to the pod. The peeled bean will slip out easily.

2. Combine the fava beans, 2 tablespoons of butter, the scallions, and ⅓ cup of water in a medium saucepan. Bring to a simmer over moderately high heat, then cover and reduce the heat. Continue simmering until the beans are tender, about 8 minutes; uncover the pot and test often for doneness. If the beans cook through before the liquid has evaporated, uncover the pot and allow the excess liquid to evaporate. Season the beans to taste with salt and pepper.

3. While the beans cook, bring the stock and the remaining tablespoon of butter to a boil in a medium saucepan. Add the couscous, stir once, cover, and remove the pot from the heat. Let it stand 5 minutes. Add the dill and gently but thoroughly fluff the grains of couscous with a fork to separate them.

4. Combine the couscous and fava beans in a warm serving bowl; toss with a fork to blend. Season to taste with salt and pepper.

NOTE: Fava beans are best when fully formed but small. Avoid large pods with bulging beans inside.

NOTE: Couscous, made from semolina (durum wheat) mixed with water and shaped into tiny dried pellets, can vary in its cooking qualities from one supplier to the next. I prefer French couscous, whether packaged or sold in bulk; in my experience, both kinds work in this recipe. The package directions on imported couscous may tell you to use more liquid than this recipe calls for, but I find that these proportions produce the fluffy texture that I like. The domestic packaged couscous will not cook up properly by this method; if you are using it, follow the directions on the package.

OTHER SERVING SUGGESTIONS

BRAISED FAVA BEANS Braise shelled and peeled favas in butter or olive oil with a little water or chicken stock. Season them with thyme, rosemary, or sage; add a little finely minced prosciutto at the end, if you like. You can also replace the butter or oil with rendered pancetta (Italian unsmoked bacon).

BRAISED FAVA BEANS WITH ESCAROLE Braise shredded escarole and fava beans in olive oil with garlic, chopped mint, and just enough water or stock to keep the vegetables from sticking.

FAVA BEAN PARTNERS Because they are so time-consuming to prepare, I usually "stretch" fava beans with other vegetables or grains (see Couscous with Fava Beans, page 50). They combine well with other shelling beans, corn, artichokes, peas, and green onions.

LEEKS

Like many Americans, I first tasted leeks in France, where they are a fixture in the French take-out shops known as *charcuteries*. You can always spot them from the window—fat green leeks on a white platter, glistening in mustard vinaigrette. When I lived with a Parisian family, the housekeeper prepared leeks often. She would poach them first, then arrange them in a buttered baking dish, drape them with sliced ham, pour a bechamel sauce over all, and heat them until browned and bubbling.

Leeks are popular throughout Europe but have never played a big role on the American table. They should. These elongated members of the onion family turn sweet and creamy when cooked; they are particularly appealing with fish.

TO SELECT   Leeks should have fresh-looking bright green leaves; a goodly portion of the leek should be white to pale green. (This is the choice part for eating. In French kitchens, the dark green part of the leaves is saved to flavor stock for soups and sauces.) Avoid leeks with splits. Choose the smaller ones; overly large leeks can be tough or woody inside.

TO STORE   Refrigerate leeks in the vegetable crisper in a perforated plastic bag. Use within 3 to 4 days.

COOKING TIPS   ***Trimming and Washing***   Leeks need to be washed well before cooking. The white part of the leek is buried in dirt to blanch it and the dirt frequently lodges between the layers. Cut off the dark green leaves; save them for stock if you like. Trim the hairy root end but don't cut it off or the leek won't hold together. Cut the leek in half lengthwise, stopping about an inch from the root end. Hold the leek under cold running water and rinse away any dirt that may be caught between the layers. Drain.

SWEET AND SOUR LEEKS

This is a great dinner party dish because it sits well; in fact, it tastes best when not hot from the skillet. I like it at room temperature; it's also good warm, but you should let it rest at least 15 minutes after cooking so the leeks can absorb the lovely sweet-sour flavors of the sauce.

Try them with fresh tuna steaks, a veal roast, roast chicken, braised tongue, or calf's liver.

Serves 4

> **4 leeks, no larger than 1 inch in diameter**
> **2 tablespoons olive oil**
> **½ medium onion, minced**
> **16-ounce can peeled tomatoes**
> **1 tablespoon brown sugar**
> **2 tablespoons lemon juice, or more to taste**
> **1 bay leaf**
> **2 cloves**
> **Salt and freshly ground black pepper**
> **1 tablespoon finely chopped fresh mint**

1. Trim and wash the leeks as directed on page 52, but slit them completely in half lengthwise instead of stopping 1 inch from the end. Pat them dry and set them aside.

2. Heat the olive oil in a heavy 10-inch skillet over moderate heat. Add the onion and saute until it softens, about 5 minutes. Add the tomatoes and their juice, crushing them between your fingers as you add them (do this carefully to avoid splattering tomato juice everywhere). Add the brown sugar, 2 tablespoons of lemon juice, the bay leaf, cloves, and salt and pepper to taste. Bring to a simmer and cook, stirring often to prevent sticking, until the sauce is quite thick, about 15 to 20 minutes.

3. Add the leeks cut side down; they should fit snugly in one layer. Cover the pan, reduce the heat to moderately low, and simmer until the leeks are just tender, about 20 minutes. Turn the heat off and cool the leeks at least 15 minutes in the skillet.

4. To serve, transfer the leeks to a platter with tongs. Remove the bay leaf and cloves from the sauce. Stir the mint into the sauce, then taste it and add more lemon juice if necessary. Spoon the sauce over the leeks.

BAKED LEEKS IN MUSTARD CREAM

A trouble-free party dish, these leeks need almost no last-minute attention. You can wash them, arrange them in the baking dish, and prepare the cream mixture ahead of time. They come out of the oven beautifully browned, meltingly soft, and slightly crisp around the edges. They will flatter a roast leg of lamb, roast chicken, fresh salmon, or broiled shrimp.

Serves 4

> **8 medium leeks, about ¾ inch in diameter**
> **½ cup chicken stock**
> **½ cup whipping cream**
> **1 tablespoon Dijon-style mustard**
> **Salt and freshly ground black pepper**
> **1 tablespoon minced parsley (optional)**

1. Preheat the oven to 375°. Trim and wash the leeks (see page 52).

2. Whisk the chicken stock, cream, and mustard together in a small bowl. Season with salt and pepper. Arrange the leeks in a shallow-sided baking dish just large enough to hold them in one layer. Pour the seasoned cream over them. Bake 30 minutes, then turn the leeks over with tongs. Continue baking, spooning the cream over the leeks once or twice, until the cream has been almost entirely absorbed and the leeks are beginning to brown and crisp, about another 30 to 35 minutes. Garnish with minced parsley if desired; serve from the baking dish.

OTHER SERVING SUGGESTIONS

LEEKS VINAIGRETTE Dress room-temperature boiled leeks with a thick mustard vinaigrette and serve as part of a grilled-chicken picnic.

GRILLED LEEKS Blanch leeks in salted water, drain well, and pat dry. Brush them with oil, and brown them on a charcoal grill.

LEEKS IN CREAM Slice leeks and soften them slightly in butter in a skillet; add cream and simmer until the leeks are soft and the cream has thickened. Freshly grated nutmeg or some minced tarragon would be a nice addition.

BRAISED LEEKS Braise whole or halved leeks in poultry or meat stock until the stock has reduced to a syrupy glaze.

PEAS

Many markets these days carry three types of fresh peas: shelling peas (also known as English peas), snow peas, and sugar snap peas. The latter two types have edible pods and are meant to be eaten whole after stringing.

I can't get enthusiastic about the English peas you find in most markets. Nine times out of ten, they're disappointing—starchy, tough, overgrown. Nothing you can do will make them taste good; you're better off with frozen petite peas.

But if you can grow them yourself, harvest them young, and cook them the day you pick them, you will taste peas as tender and sweet as they are meant to be. They will spoil you for anything less. You can also do well if you patronize a farmers' market or a retailer who buys from local sources at the time of year when peas are harvested in your area. At other times of year, forget about fresh English peas.

TO SELECT

Shelling (English) peas should have smooth, bright green pods with fully formed but not bulging peas.

Snow peas should be bright green, flexible but not limp, and moist; avoid any that are blemished or drying out along the seams.

Sugar snap peas should have a pretty bright green color. Avoid the large ones that appear to have fully formed peas inside; they will be tough.

Peas deteriorate quickly after picking and start converting their sugar to starch. Try to buy from a market that buys its supply locally and turns it over quickly.

TO STORE

It's best to use peas the day you buy them. If you must store them, keep them in a perforated plastic bag in the refrigerator vegetable crisper for no more than a day or two. Leave English peas in the shell until you are ready to use them.

COOKING TIPS

Shelling (English) Peas Shell the peas and steam them in a covered saucepan in just enough water to keep them from sticking. Depending on their age, they will take 5 to 10 minutes to cook. Drain well.

Snow Peas Snow peas take very little cooking. Stir-fry them in corn or peanut oil, adding a few drops of water or stock so that they steam a little. When they have lost their raw taste but before they turn limp, they are ready.

Sugar Snap Peas The best way to preserve the bright green color of sugar snap peas is to blanch them in boiling water until they just lose their raw taste, then drain, return them to the pot, and shake the pot over low heat until the peas dry.

PEAS AND PODS WITH TARRAGON

At the now-defunct Pig by the Tail charcuterie in Berkeley, California, proprietor Victoria Wise used to make a delicious "Peas and Pods" salad with English peas and snow peas. My variation on her clever original uses crunchy sugar snap peas and is intended to be served hot, with leg of lamb, roast chicken or duck, or baked salmon or sole.

Serves 4

> ½ **pound sugar snap peas, strings removed**
> 2 **tablespoons unsalted butter**
> ¼ **cup minced shallots**
> 1½ **cups shelled English peas (about 1½ pounds before shelling)**
> 2 **teaspoons minced fresh tarragon or chervil**
> **Salt and freshly ground black pepper**

1. Blanch the sugar snap peas in a large pot of boiling water until they just lose their raw taste (see Note); timing will depend on the size and age of the peas, but it should take about 1 to 3 minutes. Drain and rinse the peas under cold water to stop the cooking. Pat them dry.

2. Melt the butter in a 10-inch skillet over moderately low heat. Add the shallots and saute until they soften, about 3 minutes. Add the English peas and ¼ cup of water. Cover and steam until the peas are almost done, about 5 to 10 minutes, depending on their age. Uncover, add the sugar snap peas, and cook, stirring often, until they are heated through. Add the tarragon and salt and pepper to taste.

VARIATION: You could also add some quartered boiled red potatoes when you add the sugar snap peas.

NOTE: If you can find very young sugar snap peas—the kind that are tender and sweet when raw—they don't need blanching. Older ones should be blanched.

PEAS IN CREME FRAICHE

A little *crème fraîche* stirred into braised sweet peas creates an instant silky sauce. This dish is so simple, quick, and tasty that I bet you will make it often.

I don't hesitate to use frozen petite peas here; from a good packer, they are often sweeter and more tender than fresh ones. Serve this delicate dish with pork chops, roast chicken or ham, pan-fried calf's liver or chicken livers, or baked salmon.

Serves 4

> 2 cups fresh shelling peas (about 2 pounds) or frozen petite peas
> 1 tablespoon butter
> ¼ cup finely minced scallions (green onions)
> ¼ cup *crème fraîche,* whisked until smooth (see Note)
> Salt and freshly cracked black pepper (see Note)

1. *If using fresh peas,* shell them and put them in a medium saucepan with the butter, scallions, and about ¼ cup of water. Bring to a simmer over moderate heat, then cover and cook until the peas are tender. Young tender peas will take only about 3 minutes, older ones somewhat longer. When the peas are just done, uncover the pot, raise the heat, and cook until any excess liquid has evaporated.

   If using frozen peas, do not thaw them. Put them in a medium saucepan with the butter, scallions, and about 3 tablespoons of water. Cook uncovered over moderate heat, stirring often, until the peas are hot throughout and any excess liquid has evaporated.

2. Reduce the heat to low. Gently stir in the *crème fraîche* with a rubber spatula. Season to taste with salt and pepper. When the peas are hot throughout, transfer them to a warm serving bowl and serve immediately.

NOTE: *Crème fraîche,* a thick cultured cream with the texture of sour cream, is available in many cheese stores and some well-stocked supermarkets. To make your own, see the Note on page 74.

NOTE: I recommend crushing the peppercorns in a mortar so that they have a coarse texture, but you can also use ground pepper from a mill.

OTHER SERVING SUGGESTIONS

English peas mix well with so many different vegetables that when they're in season, I'm tempted to add them to everything. Combine them in a stew with one or several of the following: mushrooms, pearl onions, carrots, asparagus, artichokes, fennel, fava beans, green beans, lettuce, cucumbers, corn, okra, whole shallots, squash, turnips, or fresh water chestnuts. Aim for combinations that are colorful and compatible, like Sweet Potatoes, Parsnips, and Peas (page 139).

HERBED ENGLISH PEAS Steam and drain the peas, then stir in a knob of butter and the herbs of your choice. Tarragon, dill, chives, mint, basil, and parsley are compatible with peas. You can also add some very finely minced ham or scallion (green onion) or a little grated lemon zest.

PEAS IN CREAM Steam shelling peas until they are about half done. Add heavy cream and simmer uncovered until the cream thickens. My husband speaks fondly of a similar dish his mother used to make using her own garden peas and tiny new potatoes and cream from their cow.

BUTTERED SUGAR SNAPS Blanch the peas, drain them, and dry well; add a knob of butter and some salt and toss to coat. It is hard to imagine improving on plain buttered sugar snap peas.

SUMMER

CHARD	*Buttered Chard with Parmesan*
	Swiss Chard with Anchovy Butter
CORN	*Corn on the Cob Mexican Style*
	Polenta with Fresh Corn
	Corn and Limas
	Creamed Corn and Hominy
CUCUMBER	*Thai Cucumber Salad*
	Cucumber and Tomato Raita
EGGPLANT	*Baked Ratatouille*
	Grilled Eggplant Puree, Indian Style
	Grilled Eggplant with Yogurt Sauce
	Eggplant, Tomato, and Chick Pea Stew
GREEN BEANS	*Green Beans with Sesame Seeds*
	Green Beans and Limas with Dill
	Green Beans with Pecorino
OKRA	*Skillet Okra and Peppers*
	Indian-Style Okra with Tomatoes
PEPPERS	*Peperonata (Stewed Peppers and*
	Tomatoes, Italian Style)
	Grilled Peppers and Onions
SUMMER SQUASH	*Broiled Zucchini with Parmesan*
	Jeanne's Summer Squash
TOMATOES	*Baked Tomatoes with Feta*
	Tomato Bread Crisp
	Tomatoes with Buttermilk Dressing
	Panzanella (Tuscan Bread Salad)
	Tomatoes with Arugula Pesto

SUMMER COOKING for me means quick and uncomplicated cooking because I'd always rather be in the garden. That's why I often serve summer vegetables either raw, cool, or grilled. Those approaches seem to fit best with summer schedules and appetites.

Raw Is Easiest

Some of the best summer vegetable dishes don't even require cooking. Sliced ripe tomatoes—perhaps mixed yellow and red varieties—can simply be topped with minced herbs, olive oil, and vinegar. Thinly sliced cucumbers are delicious tossed with garlicky sour cream. Grated, salted, and squeezed-dry summer squash (see page 105) is terrific just tossed in a vinaigrette. The Panzanella on page 113 requires no cooking, nor does the cooling Cucumber and Tomato Raita on page 81.

Cool Means Refreshing

On hot days, a plate of steaming food isn't always appealing; consider serving a salad of raw or cooked and cooled vegetables instead. Many cooked vegetables actually taste better at room temperature, and you can make them more or less at your leisure. For a quick and tasty salad, toss steamed green beans with vinaigrette and garnish with a mixture of chopped eggs and olives, or dress the cooled beans with minced shallots, walnut oil, and sherry vinegar. Peeled roasted peppers sliced into strips and tossed with minced anchovies, capers, olive oil, and lemon juice make an especially colorful dish. The Baked Ratatouille on page 84 and the Grilled Eggplant with Yogurt Scallion Sauce on page 87 are perfect hot-day dishes.

When You Grill, Grill Vegetables

If you're grilling meat on a summer night, it makes sense to grill the vegetables too. Eggplant, squash, and peppers perform beautifully on the grill. See Grilled Eggplant Puree, Indian Style (page 86) for directions on grilling a whole globe eggplant; for a quick and delicious vegetable dish, peel and mash a whole grilled eggplant, drain the puree in a sieve, then season it with olive oil, garlic, lemon juice, and toasted cumin. To grill halved Asian eggplants or eggplant slices, see Grilled Eggplant with Yogurt Scallion Sauce (page 87). The recipe for Grilled Peppers and Onions on page 103 will teach you how to roast peppers on the grill. To grill zucchini or crookneck squashes, cut them in half lengthwise, brush with olive oil, and cook slowly on a relatively cool part of the grill. Alternatively, squash can be steamed lightly before grilling to shorten the grilling time. Steam zucchini or crookneck squashes whole, then cut them in half, brush with oil, and cook over a brisk fire.

Some of the year-round vegetables on pages 192 through 220 make appealing summer side dishes when grilled. Grilled Mushroom Caps (page 206) with a grilled flank steak, or Doug's Grilled New Potatoes (page 215) with grilled fish and a garlic mayonnaise come to mind as happy marriages. In *taquerías* in San Francisco's Hispanic Mission district I've enjoyed whole scallions brushed with oil, grilled until brown, then sprinkled with coarse salt.

CHARD

Often called Swiss chard (a name food historians are at a loss to explain), chard belongs in that category of leafy greens suited to cooking, along with kale, collard greens, mustard greens, turnip greens, and beet greens. Unlike the others, however, chard can tolerate hot weather; thus, it's the green you're most likely to find in the best shape in summer markets.

Chard seems to me to have a more delicate flavor than any of the other greens mentioned above. It can take aggressive seasoning but it doesn't need it. In fact, when you can find some young chard, you can't do better than to blanch the leaves until they are just tender, drain them well, then dress them with extra virgin olive oil and coarse salt. Both white-ribbed and red-ribbed varieties can be handled in the same way.

TO SELECT   Look for greens with a fresh, crisp appearance; the ribs should be firm and unblemished.

TO STORE   Refrigerate in a perforated plastic bag. Chard will keep for a couple of days.

COOKING TIPS   Very young leaves (which you are unlikely to find unless you grow them yourself) may be eaten raw in salads. Older leaves need cooking, either by steaming in just the water clinging to the leaves after washing or by boiling briefly in a large quantity of salted water. Because the ribs take longer to cook than the leaves, it is best to remove them and cook them separately; boil them first until just tender, then chop and reheat them with butter or olive oil. Red chard ribs will lose some of their color when boiled. Sometimes the ribs are cracked and browned and not even worth salvaging.

BUTTERED CHARD WITH PARMESAN

Here's how Italians cook full-flavored greens—steaming them briefly to wilt them, then warming them through with garlic. You can use olive oil if you like, but I prefer the nutty taste of butter here.

If the chard ribs are fresh-looking and unblemished, save them and use them the next day.

Serves 4

> 1½ **pounds chard**
> 3 **tablespoons butter**
> 2 **cloves garlic, minced**
> **Salt and freshly ground black pepper**
> **Parmesan cheese**

1. Wash the chard well and drain it, but do not pat it dry. Trim away the ribs (see illustration).

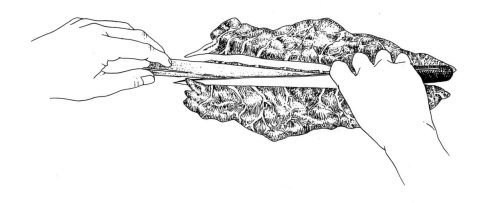

2. Put the leaves in a large pot with just the water clinging to them. Cover the pot and set it over moderate heat. Steam just until the leaves wilt, about 3 to 5 minutes; uncover the pot once or twice during cooking and toss the leaves with tongs to make sure they wilt evenly. Cool the leaves in a colander under cold running water to stop the cooking. When cool, squeeze the leaves between your palms to release excess moisture. Chop coarsely.

3. Melt the butter in a saucepan over moderately low heat. Add the garlic and saute until fragrant, about 1 minute. Add the chard and salt and pepper to taste (remember that you will also be adding Parmesan, which is salty). Toss to coat the leaves with butter and cook until heated through. Transfer to a warm serving bowl or platter. Grate Parmesan thickly over the surface.

SWISS CHARD WITH ANCHOVY BUTTER

This dish is perhaps prettier made with red chard but it's equally tasty made with green. Use red wine vinegar with red chard, white wine vinegar with green chard. Chicken, pork, or veal would be good companions—perhaps some pan-fried Italian fennel sausage, roast pork tenderloins, a stuffed veal breast, or broiled chicken halves seasoned with rosemary.

Serves 4 generously

> 1½ **pounds chard, red or green (see Note)**
> 12 **whole black peppercorns**
> 2 **anchovy fillets**
> 3 **tablespoons unsalted butter, softened**
> 1 **tablespoon wine vinegar, or more to taste**
> **Salt**

1. Wash the chard well and drain it but do not pat it dry. Trim away the ribs (see illustration, left) and set them aside.

2. Put the leaves in a large pot with just the water clinging to them. Cover the pot and set it over moderate heat. Steam the leaves just until wilted, about 3 to 5 minutes; uncover the pot once or twice during cooking and toss the leaves with tongs to make sure they wilt evenly. Drain the leaves in a colander (they will not give off much liquid). When cool, chop coarsely.

69

3. Put the peppercorns in a mortar and pound them with a pestle until coarsely ground. Add the anchovy fillets and pound until reduced to a paste. Add 2 tablespoons of butter and stir until well blended. Set aside.

4. Slice the chard ribs crosswise into ½-inch pieces (if the ribs are more than about ¾ inch wide, cut them in half lengthwise first). Heat the remaining tablespoon of butter in a large skillet over moderate heat. Add the chard ribs and 1 tablespoon of vinegar; season to taste with salt. Stir to coat the ribs with butter, then cover, reduce the heat to moderately low, and cook until the ribs are tender, about 10 to 15 minutes.

5. Uncover the pan, raise the heat to moderate, and add the chard leaves. Cook, stirring, until the chard is hot throughout and any excess liquid has evaporated. Remove from the heat and stir in the anchovy butter. Season to taste with salt and add more vinegar if desired. Serve immediately.

NOTE: Look for chard with pretty ribs, as you are going to use them.

OTHER SERVING SUGGESTIONS

STEAMED CHARD VINAIGRETTE Steam chard leaves in a covered pot in just the water clinging to them after washing; drain thoroughly, then dress them with olive oil, salt, pepper, and lemon juice or vinegar.

CHARD WITH ONIONS AND BACON Boil the leaves and ribs separately; drain, pat dry, and chop coarsely. Render some diced bacon or pancetta (Italian unsmoked bacon) then saute some chopped onions and garlic in the pork fat. Add the chopped chard and reheat.

CHARD RIBS WITH GARLIC AND PARMESAN Cut the ribs into bite-size pieces and boil them in salted water until tender. Drain, pat dry, and reheat in butter with a little minced garlic, salt, and pepper. Garnish with grated Parmesan.

CHARD WITH WHITE BEANS OR LENTILS Stir chopped boiled chard into a pot of stewed white beans or lentils.

CORN

It's hard to believe that the French and Italians—such appreciators of good food—don't grow and enjoy sweet corn. It is surely one of this country's favorite vegetables. There may not be a more beloved American side dish than buttered corn on the cob, although I hope you will venture beyond that to some of the recipes in this section. Corn combines beautifully with other grains and beans. I also particularly like combinations of fresh and dried corn—fresh corn in spoonbread, with hominy, or in polenta.

TO SELECT

Freshness is the most important factor in choosing sweet corn because the sugar in corn starts converting to starch as soon as it is harvested. Corn breeders have developed new strains that are very slow to convert sugar to starch. These supersweet varieties do stay sweet longer, but most of them have an intense, almost candylike sweetness that I don't enjoy. If they are identified as supersweet I avoid them, although I know that many shoppers seek them out.

You can tell fresh corn by the appearance of the stem end (it should be moist and pale green) and the tassel (the stringy part at the tip of the ear), which gets brown and mushy when the corn has been off the stalk for a while. The tip of the cob should also be firm, not mushy. The kernels should look plump and should be milky when pierced. Produce managers may not like it, but I usually strip some of the husk to inspect the kernels and pierce one if I have any doubts.

TO STORE

Buy corn the day you plan to eat it and refrigerate it in the husk. If the grocer has removed all or part of the husk, store the ears in a perforated plastic bag.

COOKING TIPS
On the Cob

Boiling Bring a large pot of unsalted water to a boil (salt toughens the kernels). Husk the corn just before cooking, removing all the silky strings. Drop the ears into the boiling water, cover, and remove from the heat. Let stand 5 minutes, then drain. Older corn and extra-large ears will take slightly longer, very fresh young corn slightly less.

Grilling Prepare a moderate charcoal fire. Peel back but do not remove the husks. Remove and discard the corn silk. Put the husks back in place and tie them at the tip with string. Soak the corn in cold water for 10 minutes to moisten the husks, then drain. Grill over the coals until tender, about 15 minutes; turn often.

Off the Cob Remove the husks and silk. Cut off the stem and set the ear upright on its base. With a sharp knife, slice straight down the length of the cob, cutting off a few rows of kernels at a time. Saute the kernels in butter over moderately low heat until cooked through, about 5 to 10 minutes. (Older corn takes longer than young corn.) Season with salt and pepper.

CORN ON THE COB MEXICAN STYLE

If you think butter and salt are the only proper condiments for corn, think again. Boiled corn slathered with thick cream and ground chile is sold from street carts all over Mexico, and it is hard to resist. If you live near a Mexican market, you may be able to find thick Mexican *crema*. If not, substitute French *crème fraîche*; it's available in many cheese stores, or you can make your own (see Note, page 74).

Serves 4

> 4 ears fresh corn, shucked
> 6 to 8 tablespoons *crème fraîche*, whisked
> Salt
> Chili powder
> Lime wedges (optional)

1. Bring a large pot of water to a boil over high heat. Add the corn, cover the pot, and remove it from the heat. Let stand 5 minutes.

2. Season the *crème fraîche* to taste with salt. When the corn is ready, remove it from the pot with tongs and let the excess water drip back into the pot. Using a rubber spatula, spread each ear generously with cream (the larger the ears, the more cream you will need) then sprinkle liberally with chili powder; add a squeeze of lime if you like. Serve immediately.

Corn on the Cob Mexican Style

NOTE: To make *crème fraîche*, put 1 cup of heavy cream (not ultrapasteurized) in a saucepan and heat over low heat until it is just lukewarm (about 100°). Put the cream in a clean lidded glass jar. Add 1 tablespoon of buttermilk, cover, and shake for 1 minute. Let the jar stand at room temperature until the cream thickens, 12 to 24 hours. Refrigerate when thick. It will keep for at least a week.

POLENTA WITH FRESH CORN

A pool of soft polenta studded with fresh corn kernels would flatter almost any meat from a charcoal grill: Italian sausages, quail, spareribs, chops. Or top the polenta with grilled skewered sausage chunks and peppers. Sometimes I pour it out onto a wooden cutting board and serve it from the board, family style; it firms up as it cools.

This is an unconventional way to cook polenta. Most recipe writers tell you to add the polenta to the boiling water; for this recipe I do it the other way around because it's easier and it works.

Serves 6

> **3 tablespoons butter**
> **2 cups corn kernels (about 2 large or 3 small ears)**
> **1 cup polenta**
> **2½ cups chicken broth mixed with 2½ cups water, simmering,**
>   **plus more as needed**
> **Salt and freshly ground black pepper**

Melt 2 tablespoons of butter in a 3-quart saucepan over moderate heat. Add the corn and saute 2 minutes. Add the polenta and stir to coat it with butter. Add 5 cups of the hot broth mixture gradually, stirring constantly with a wooden spoon. Bring to a simmer, reduce the heat, and continue simmering, stirring often, until the mixture is thick, smooth, and no longer gritty, about 40 minutes. If necessary, add additional boiling stock or water. Just before serving, stir in the remaining tablespoon of butter and season to taste with salt and pepper.

CORN AND LIMAS

This is one of my favorite side dishes—fat limas and sweet corn in a rich pork-flavored broth. I would serve it with roast chicken, duck, or game birds, roast pork loin or braised pork shoulder, spareribs, meat loaf, or baked salmon. If you don't like limas, try it with other dried beans such as kidney beans, flageolets, or blackeyed peas.

Serves 4

> 1 cup dried lima beans
> 8 ounces smoked pork hock or slab bacon, in two pieces
> ½ onion stuck with 1 clove
> 3 cloves garlic, peeled
> 1 bay leaf
> 2 cups fresh corn kernels (about 2 large or 3 small ears)
> ½ red bell pepper, minced
> Salt and freshly ground black pepper

1. Soak the beans overnight in cold water 2 inches deeper than the beans; drain. *To quick soak:* Put the beans in a pot; fill with cold water to 2 inches above the beans. Bring to a boil and boil 1 minute, then cover and set aside 2 hours; drain.

2. Put the drained beans in a 4-quart saucepan; add 5 cups of cold water. Add the pork, onion, garlic, and bay leaf. Bring to a simmer over moderate heat, lower the heat, and continue simmering until the beans are tender but not mushy, about 1½ hours. The beans should be neither dry nor soupy; there should be just enough cooking liquid left to moisten them. If the liquid reduces too much during cooking, cover the pot partially or add a little boiling water.

3. Remove the pork, onion, and bay leaf. Stir in the corn and red pepper. Cover and cook over moderately low heat, stirring gently a couple of times, until the corn is cooked, about 10 minutes. Uncover and season to taste with salt and pepper.

CREAMED CORN AND HOMINY

Fresh and dried corn cooked together in chile-spiked cream—so simple, so good. I first tasted this dish with grilled lamb chops and have made it many times since. It would flatter a baked ham, pork chops, or a pork shoulder cooked slowly on the grill over some hickory chips. Like all chiles, jalapeños vary a lot in strength. Start with half a seeded jalapeño, then, if you want more heat, add more, or throw in the seeds.

Serves 4

> **14½-ounce can white or golden hominy (see Note)**
> **1 cup heavy cream**
> **1 cup chicken stock**
> **½ jalapeño chile, seeded if desired, minced**
> **1 bay leaf**
> **1 small clove garlic, minced**
> **2 cups corn kernels (about 2 large or 3 small ears)**
> **Salt and freshly ground black pepper**
> **2 tablespoons minced fresh coriander (cilantro), optional**

1. Drain the hominy and rinse it under cold running water. Put it in a 3-quart saucepan with the cream, chicken stock, chile, bay leaf, and garlic. Bring to a simmer, lower the heat, and continue simmering until the cream has reduced and thickened considerably, about 20 minutes.

2. Stir in the corn. Cover and cook until the corn is done, about 10 minutes. The cream should be reduced to a delicious thick sauce; if it is too thin, cook uncovered, stirring often, until it thickens. Season to taste with salt and a good deal of pepper; remove the bay leaf. Transfer to a warm serving bowl and garnish with coriander.

NOTE: If you prefer, you can use fresh-cooked hominy. Soak a scant cup of dried white or yellow corn kernels overnight in a large saucepan with water to cover. Drain in a sieve and return the corn to the saucepan with fresh water to cover. Bring to a boil and stir in ¼ teaspoon of slaked lime (calcium hydroxide, available from Latin markets that manufacture tortillas). Boil 10 minutes, then cover and set aside 30 minutes. Rinse the corn very well under cold running water, rubbing it between your fingers to remove any loosened papery outer skin.

It is optional but desirable to pinch off the dark germ at the base of each kernel; removing the germ allows the kernel to open up nicely as it cooks. After doing so, rinse the kernels again and put them in a saucepan with 4 cups of water. Bring to a boil, reduce the heat, cover, and simmer until tender, 1 to 1½ hours, adding more water if necessary. Drain and use as desired. You will have about 2 cups hominy.

OTHER SERVING SUGGESTIONS

BUTTERED CORN ON THE COB Fresh boiled corn on the cob needs nothing but butter and salt. If you want a change of pace, season the butter with minced fresh herbs, such as parsley, chives, chive blossoms, or chervil.

CORN ON THE COB WITH CHILE BUTTER Stir some finely minced chiles and cilantro into whipped butter and spread it on boiled corn on the cob.

CORN ON THE COB SOUTH AMERICAN STYLE In South America chunks of boiled corn about 1½ inches wide are often served as a garnish for appetizers and entrees. This is a good way to serve corn when you suspect people may not want a whole ear—as part of a buffet, for example, with a lot of other food. Just slice boiled corn across the cob into 1½-inch widths, then pile the chunks in a warm bowl and drizzle them with salted melted butter.

SAUTEED CORN WITH SWEET PEPPERS Saute corn kernels slowly in butter with finely minced scallions and diced red and green bell peppers.

STEWED CORN, TOMATOES, ZUCCHINI, AND BASIL Stew chopped tomatoes in butter or olive oil with fresh basil leaves until the tomatoes are reduced to a sauce. Add sliced or diced zucchini and corn kernels and cook until both are tender.

CORN WITH OKRA Steam okra and slice it, then combine it with corn kernels that have been sauteed slowly in butter until tender. If you wish, add some chopped red bell pepper or a little minced red chile to the corn as you saute it.

CUCUMBER

Crisp, cool, juicy cucumbers make inviting side dishes in warm weather. I especially like the refreshing crunch of a cucumber salad at picnics, barbecues, and other outdoor meals.

The long hothouse English cucumbers and the specialty Japanese and Armenian cucumbers that you find in some produce markets in the summer are a big improvement over common green cucumbers, which are too often overgrown, overly seedy, and bitter. Seek out these tastier specimens or grow them yourself to get cucumbers that are worth being made into side dishes.

TO SELECT
Cucumbers should be firm and not overlarge. Green cucumbers should be fully green, with no yellowing, which indicates overmaturity. Avoid any that are shriveled or soft in spots.

TO STORE
Cucumbers don't like to be too cold. Refrigerate them in the door storage area, which is the warmest part of most refrigerators. If their skin isn't waxed, keep cucumbers in a plastic bag. Cucumbers do not keep well; try to use them within 2 to 3 days.

COOKING TIPS
Although they're not high on my list, cooked cucumbers can be appealing with delicate fish, such as sole or turbot. Peel the cucumbers, halve them lengthwise, and remove any seeds by scraping the seed cavity with a small spoon. Cut the cucumber into slices or batons (thick strips) or neat cubes, then saute in butter until tender; season with salt and pepper.

THAI CUCUMBER SALAD

Hot, sweet, tart, and cooling flavors coalesce in this salad, with the added pungency of lemongrass and Thai fish sauce. If you have eaten in Thai restaurants, you have probably had something comparable. In a Western meal, it would offer a refreshing counterpoint to grilled salmon or sea bass or to thin-sliced pork chops seasoned with a paste of black pepper and garlic, then grilled.

Serves 4 to 6

> **1 English cucumber (about 1 pound)**
> **½ red onion**
> **1 stalk lemongrass (see Note)**
> **¼ cup coarsely chopped fresh mint**
> **3 tablespoons lime juice**
> **½ tablespoon sugar**
> **1½ tablespoons Thai fish sauce (see Note)**
> **1 small fresh red chile, halved, seeded if desired, and finely sliced**
> **¼ cup coarsely chopped roasted peanuts**

1. Remove and discard the ends of the cucumber; slice the cucumber in half lengthwise. Lay the halves cut side down and cut them crosswise into thin slices. Transfer the slices to a large bowl.

2. Slice the onion as thinly as possible; put about half of the slices in the bowl with the cucumber. (You don't need the other half, but cutting an onion half is much easier than cutting an onion quarter.)

3. Cut away the tough root end of the lemongrass and discard the outer leaf layer. Slice about 2 inches of the stalk into the finest possible rounds; use your fingers to separate the rounds into fine rings. Add them to the bowl along with the mint, lime juice, sugar, fish sauce, and half of the chile. Toss to blend. Let stand 15 minutes, then taste and adjust the seasoning, adding more chile if desired. Use a slotted spoon to transfer the salad to a serving dish; top with the peanuts.

NOTE: Both Thai fish sauce (*nam pla*) and lemongrass are available in many Asian markets. Lemongrass looks something like a large scallion or a skinny leek, but it is stiff and somewhat woody. It has a pleasant lemon-like taste.

CUCUMBER AND TOMATO RAITA

Indians serve yogurt-based *raita* as a cooling counterpoint to spicy foods. This version will fit right into a Western meal, as a partner to grilled sausages, grilled salmon, or a peppery grilled game hen. The richer the yogurt you use, the better the dish will be.

Serves 4

> 1½ cups plain yogurt, preferably whole-milk
> 1 tablespoon vegetable oil
> ¾-inch knob fresh ginger
> 1½ cups seeded and chopped tomatoes
> ¼ teaspoon cayenne pepper, or to taste
> ¼ teaspoon ground toasted cumin, or to taste (see Note)
> 1 medium English cucumber (12 ounces)
> Salt

1. Whisk the yogurt in a large bowl. Whisk in the oil. Peel the ginger and grate it into a small bowl, discarding the stringy parts. Add 1 teaspoon of grated ginger to the yogurt along with the tomatoes, cayenne, and cumin. Stir to blend. You can make the dish up to this point one hour ahead and refrigerate it.

2. Peel the cucumber. Halve it lengthwise and scrape out the seeds. Using the largest holes on the grater, grate the cucumber directly into the yogurt mixture. Season to taste with salt. Serve immediately. (The cucumber tends to thin out the yogurt as it stands.)

NOTE: Toast about ½ teaspoon whole cumin seeds in a small dry skillet over moderately low heat until fragrant and lightly browned. Shake the skillet often; do not allow the seeds to burn. Pound the seeds to a powder in a mortar or grind them in a spice grinder, then measure out the amount you need.

Indian-Style Okra with Tomatoes (page 98),
bottom: Cucumber and Tomato Raita

OTHER SERVING SUGGESTIONS

HERBED CUCUMBERS Add a squeeze of lemon and some minced fresh dill, tarragon, mint, or chives to cucumbers sauteed in butter. If you want a creamy dish, add some heavy cream and reduce it over high heat until thick, or reduce the heat to low and stir in some whisked sour cream at the end. The sour cream should not boil.

SWEDISH CUCUMBER SALAD In summer, when cucumbers are at their peak of availability and goodness, they make a delicious crisp salad to pair with grilled salmon or lamb. Slice the cucumbers as thin as possible and sprinkle with a little sugar, salt, rice vinegar, and fresh minced dill.

CUCUMBERS IN SOUR CREAM Toss paper-thin cucumber slices with sour cream flavored with grated horseradish, or season the sour cream with some minced garlic and chives.

GREEK SALAD On a pretty platter layer slices of peeled and seeded raw cucumber, tomato, red onion, and fresh basil leaves, then crumble some feta cheese on top and drizzle with vinaigrette. Serve with grilled leg of lamb.

EGGPLANT

You could write a fascinating cookbook on eggplant alone, investigating the many ways this versatile vegetable is prepared around the world. Studying the particular methods and ingredients that a cook brings to eggplant can give you a good clue to a whole cuisine. Eggplant's typical companions include saffron and tomatoes in Spain; tomatoes, garlic, and basil in France; yogurt and mint in the Middle East; cumin, tomatoes, and chiles in India. The recipes in this section provide just a glimpse of the vast international repertoire of dishes made with eggplant.

TO SELECT Eggplants come in an astonishing variety of shapes, sizes, and colors, ranging from round white ones no bigger than large grapes to the hefty purple globe eggplants that are best known among Western cooks. Many markets now sell long, slender eggplants ranging in color from pale violet to inky purple and labeled variously as Chinese, Japanese, Asian, or Italian. The eggplant recipes in this book specify the type required.

Regardless of the type of eggplant, look for smooth, shiny, blemish-free skin, with no soft spots or shriveled areas.

TO STORE   Stored in a cool, dark place, eggplants will keep for a couple
                  of days. If you don't have a cool place, refrigerate them but use
                  them within a day or two.

COOKING TIPS   Eggplant can be baked, sauteed, broiled, grilled, or braised in
                  a sauce. Its delicate taste makes it a good sponge for stronger
                  flavors. Depending on how and how long it's cooked, it can
                  assume a range of textures, from slightly spongy to creamy to
                  soft and silky. It has few calories, but it's notorious for soaking
                  up oil. A chief challenge in cooking it is to make it delicious
                  without resorting to massive amounts of oil.

                  Baking   Baking eggplant whole in a 400° oven or a covered
                  charcoal grill softens the flesh to a near-puree. Before baking,
                  prick the eggplant in three or four places with a fork to allow
                  steam to escape. If you're going to bake it in the oven, put it
                  on a tray or in a baking dish. A 1-pound eggplant will take about
                  45 minutes. For instructions for baking eggplant in a charcoal
                  grill, see Grilled Eggplant Puree, Indian Style (page 86).

                  Broiling or Grilling   Broiling or grilling requires some oil, but
                  much less than frying. Slice the eggplants however you like.
                  Large eggplants can be sliced into rounds or into lengthwise
                  slices. Slices should be about ½ inch thick as they shrink in
                  cooking and thinner slices burn too easily. Japanese and Chi-
                  nese eggplants are usually sliced in half lengthwise; to make
                  them sit steady on a grill or broiler pan, cut a small slice off
                  the rounded side. Salt the slices well. (Salting draws out excess
                  moisture and keeps the eggplant from absorbing quite as much
                  oil as it would otherwise.) Let them stand 30 minutes, then
                  wipe them dry with paper towels. Arrange the slices on a tray,
                  brush them with olive oil, then turn them and brush the other
                  side. Grill or broil, turning once, until tender. Don't cook them
                  too close to the broiler or over too hot a charcoal fire or they
                  will blacken before they cook through; a moderately slow
                  approach is better. If necessary, put them closer to the broiler
                  or move them directly over the hot part of the charcoal fire
                  at the end to color them.

BAKED RATATOUILLE

This method is so much easier than most ratatouille recipes that you may never make it another way again. There's no sauteing, no peeling and seeding tomatoes. Everything goes into one baking dish, then straightaway into the oven where, in essence, the ratatouille makes itself. This is a wonderful picnic or potluck dish because it's best at room temperature; it's also best when made a day ahead. Lamb is the traditional partner for ratatouille, but it would also be lovely with grilled tuna or swordfish.

Serves 4 generously

> **1 pound Japanese eggplant, in ¾-inch cubes**
> **½ pound zucchini, in ¾-inch cubes**
> **1 green and 1 red bell pepper, seeds and ribs removed, in ¾-inch squares**
> **1 onion, coarsely chopped**
> **1 pound tomatoes, each cored and cut into 6 wedges**
> **1 tablespoon minced garlic**
> **2 teaspoons minced fresh oregano**
> **2 teaspoons minced fresh thyme**
> **1½ teaspoons salt**
> **¼ cup olive oil**
> **2 tablespoons coarsely chopped capers**
> **24 black olives, pitted**
> **¼ cup minced parsley**
> **Red wine vinegar, to taste**

1. Preheat the oven to 375°. In a large bowl, combine the eggplant, zucchini, green and red peppers, onion, tomatoes, garlic, oregano, thyme, salt, and olive oil. Toss to blend, then transfer the mixture to a large baking dish, preferably earthenware. Cover and bake 1 hour, then uncover and bake 1 more hour. Stir gently with a spatula a couple of times during the final hour. Let cool completely.

2. Just before serving, stir in the capers, olives, parsley, and vinegar. Reseason to taste with salt.

GRILLED EGGPLANT PUREE, INDIAN STYLE

Indian restaurants with a *tandoor* (clay oven) often use it for roasting eggplants. The smoky eggplant puree is then simmered in a spicy tomato sauce to make *baigan bharta*, a dish I love. In my experience, no two versions of *baigan bharta* taste the same; many chefs add peas and all of them use a complex blend of spices that varies from cook to cook.

Here's my attempt to recreate this exquisite North Indian dish. For lack of a tandoor I use a charcoal grill, with what I consider to be fine results. It is difficult to give exact seasoning measurements because so much depends on the source and freshness of your spices. You can always add more at the end, but be sure to cook the dish a few minutes afterward to mellow the spices.

Because you'll have the grill going anyway, use it to cook your meat—perhaps some chicken breasts, swordfish steaks, or lamb chops.

Serves 4

> **Two 1-pound or one 2-pound globe eggplant**
> **1 teaspoon cumin seeds**
> **⅓ cup vegetable oil**
> **3 cloves garlic, minced**
> **1 tablespoon grated fresh ginger**
> **1 cup chopped onion**
> **1 jalapeño chile, minced**
> **2½ cups chopped fresh tomatoes (no need to peel)**
> **1½ teaspoons finely ground *garam masala* (see Note)**
> **½ teaspoon turmeric**
> **Salt**
> **Cayenne pepper, to taste (optional)**
> **3 to 4 tablespoons minced fresh coriander (cilantro)**

1. Prepare a medium-hot charcoal fire. Cook the eggplant whole over the coals, with the grill covered but the vents open, until the eggplant is blackened on all sides and soft within. You will need to turn it a couple of times to blacken it all over. A 2-pound eggplant will take about 30 minutes over a moderate fire, smaller eggplants slightly less. When cool enough to handle, peel away the skin; it should lift off easily as the eggplant cools and the flesh separates from the skin. Put the eggplant flesh in a sieve, mash it lightly with a wooden spoon, and let it drain.

2. Toast the cumin seeds in a small dry skillet over moderately low heat until fragrant and lightly browned. Do not allow them to burn. Pound the seeds to a powder in a mortar or grind them in a spice grinder.

3. Heat the vegetable oil in a large heavy skillet over moderate heat. Add the garlic and ginger and saute until fragrant, about 30 seconds. Add the onion and saute, stirring often, until softened, about 5 to 8 minutes. Add the jalapeño and saute 1 minute. Add the tomatoes, *garam masala*, turmeric, and ½ teaspoon ground cumin. Cook, stirring constantly, until the tomatoes have cooked down nearly to a puree and have created a thick sauce, about 10 minutes. The mixture should be quite dry. Stir in the eggplant. Cook, stirring constantly, for 5 minutes. Season to taste with salt; if you want the dish spicier, add cayenne pepper to taste. Adjust the other seasonings to taste. When the mixture is seasoned to your liking, stir in the fresh coriander.

NOTE: *Garam masala*, an Indian spice blend, is available in Indian markets. Some markets offer it both ground and as whole mixed spices. If you have a spice grinder, buy the whole mixed spices and grind the mixture as needed.

GRILLED EGGPLANT WITH YOGURT SCALLION SAUCE

The creamy, garlicky sauce in this dish takes all of five minutes to make. I love it slathered on warm grilled eggplant; it's also great on sliced tomatoes, baked potatoes, steamed green beans, or asparagus.

You can use thick-sliced globe eggplants if you don't mind the tough skin. I prefer the long, slender Asian eggplants of 4 to 6 ounces apiece; one eggplant, halved lengthwise, makes a pretty portion.

Serves 4

Yogurt Scallion Sauce
¼ cup plain nonfat yogurt
¼ cup sour cream
1 clove garlic, finely minced
2 tablespoons finely minced scallions (green onions)
1 tablespoon minced fresh coriander (cilantro)
Salt and freshly ground black pepper
❀

4 Japanese or Chinese eggplants, about 4 to 6 inches each
Salt
Approximately 2 tablespoons olive oil
2 tablespoons minced fresh coriander (cilantro) *or* **coriander sprigs for garnish**

1. Combine all the sauce ingredients in a bowl and whisk to blend. Taste and adjust the seasoning. Set aside.

2. Halve the eggplants lengthwise through the stem, but do not remove the stem. Lay the halves cut side up on a rack or baking sheet and salt them liberally. Let them stand 30 minutes to draw out excess moisture, then wipe them dry with paper towels.

3. While the eggplants stand, prepare a moderate charcoal fire (too hot a fire will burn the eggplants before they cook through). When the coals are ready, brush the cut sides of the eggplants with oil and put them oiled side down on the grill over the coals. Cook, watching carefully, until they are lightly browned and slightly softened, about 10 to 15 minutes; if they are cooking too fast, move them to a cooler part of the grill.

4. Turn the halves over and continue cooking until the skin side is slightly crisped and the flesh is cooked through but not mushy, about 5 minutes. Transfer the eggplants to a serving platter. Spread sauce generously over each half. Let them stand 15 minutes, then garnish with coriander and serve.

EGGPLANT, TOMATO, AND CHICK PEA STEW

These three ingredients appear together in countless dishes around the world, although the seasoning changes from country to country. This recipe has an Italian accent. For an Indian flavor, add some finely minced or grated ginger, some ground cumin and turmeric, and substitute fresh coriander for the parsley. For a Spanish twist, use saffron instead of oregano, add some crumbled chorizo, and use fresh coriander in place of parsley. Experiment and enjoy this lusty dish with lamb or pork chops, a simple roast or grilled chicken, or some fresh grilled tuna.

Note that the stew tastes best at room temperature; let it cool before serving, or make it a day ahead and bring it to room temperature before serving.

Serves 6

¾ cup dried *or* 1½ cups canned chick peas (garbanzo beans)
½ onion stuck with 2 cloves (optional)
1 bay leaf (optional)
3 tablespoons olive oil
1 large onion, chopped
1 green bell pepper, chopped
2 cloves garlic, minced
2 pounds ripe tomatoes, cored and chopped
Pinch of hot red pepper flakes
1½ tablespoons minced fresh oregano
¾ pound Japanese or Chinese eggplant, in ¾-inch cubes
Salt
¼ cup minced parsley

1. If using dried chick peas, soak them overnight in cold water to cover, then drain. Place them in a saucepan with cold water 1 inch deeper than the peas. Add the onion stuck with cloves and the bay leaf. Bring to a simmer over high heat, then cover partially, reduce the heat, and simmer until the chick peas are tender, about 1½ hours, adding more hot water if necessary. Drain, discarding the onion and bay leaf. If using canned chick peas, rinse and drain them.

2. Heat the olive oil in a large, heavy skillet over moderate heat. Add the chopped onion and bell pepper and saute until softened, about 10 minutes. Add the garlic and saute until fragrant, about 1 minute. Add the tomatoes and their juices and the hot pepper flakes. Raise the heat to moderately high and cook, stirring often with a wooden spoon, until the tomatoes are reduced to a thick sauce, about 15 to 20 minutes (be careful not to let the mixture scorch).

3. Add the oregano, eggplant, chick peas, and salt to taste. Cover and simmer over low heat until the eggplant is tender, about 20 to 30 minutes. Uncover occasionally and stir gently to make sure the sauce is not sticking to the bottom of the pan. When the eggplant is tender but not mushy, remove the skillet from the heat and let the stew cool to room temperature. Taste again and reseason. Stir in the parsley just before serving.

OTHER SERVING SUGGESTIONS

EGGPLANT-TOMATO PUREE Bake a whole large eggplant until very soft inside. Cut it in half and scrape the flesh away from the skin. Drain and mash the flesh, then add a few spoonfuls of thick tomato sauce seasoned with onion and green bell pepper. Serve at room temperature with grilled lamb.

BROILED OR GRILLED EGGPLANT Spread the cooked slices lightly with pesto (see page 116), or dust them with Parmesan cheese, or shower them with grated feta cheese and minced parsley.

GREEN BEANS

Because most commercial growers have switched to stringless varieties of green beans, the term "string beans" is giving way to "snap beans." Whatever they're called, green beans are so plentiful and inexpensive that most of us eat them often. As much as I enjoy them simply buttered or dressed with oil, I sometimes want to give them a little more dimension, especially when the meat I'm serving them with is simple and sauceless—like a grilled lamb chop or a baked fish fillet.

TO SELECT	Green beans should look fresh and relatively blemish free. French *haricots verts* should be truly skinny and tender (go ahead: taste one); as they get larger, they get tough. When buying the slender Blue Lake types or the sturdy, flat Kentucky Wonder or Romano beans, look for crispness—the beans should snap when broken—and the soft, almost velvety touch of fresh-picked beans. If the seeds have started to swell in the seed pods, the beans are too mature.
TO STORE	Beans do not like to be too cold. Refrigerate them in a perforated plastic bag in the door storage area, which is the warmest part of most refrigerators. Use within 2 to 3 days.

COOKING TIPS

Boiling   Wash the beans. Pinch off the tips. (On very young beans you don't have to remove the tail end.) Boil, uncovered, in a large quantity of salted water until just tender. Drain. Dry the beans before dressing by returning them to the pot and shaking it over low heat until all the water has evaporated.

My mother was part of a generation that cooked beans until they fell apart at the touch of a fork. The trend now is to the other extreme, cooking beans so briefly that they still squeak when you eat them. I prefer a happy medium, beans that still have texture but have lost that raw green bean taste. Watch carefully and taste the boiling beans often to catch them at just the right moment.

Steaming   Steaming beans in a steamer over boiling salted water retains more of the nutrients but it takes longer than boiling, with no flavor advantages. I usually boil my beans instead.

Braising   You can braise beans, covered, in a moist medium like tomato sauce or a little chicken stock. Slender green beans can be braised raw, but larger ones should be blanched first in boiling salted water to soften them slightly. Braised beans do not keep their bright green color.

91

GREEN BEANS WITH SESAME SEEDS

If you're planning a meal with a Chinese or Japanese flavor, these nutty beans would be a good choice. A roast chicken rubbed with soy sauce and sesame oil comes to mind, or grilled flank steak in a teriyaki marinade.

Serves 6

>   1½ tablespoons sesame seeds
>   1 pound green beans, ends trimmed (see Note)
>   1 tablespoon Chinese or Japanese sesame oil
>   3 tablespoons minced fresh coriander (cilantro)
>   Salt

1. Toast the sesame seeds in a small dry skillet over low heat, shaking the skillet often or stirring until the seeds are golden brown. Go slowly and be careful; the seeds can burn quickly once they start to brown. Set aside.

2. Bring a large pot of heavily salted water to a boil. Add the green beans and cook rapidly until done; timing will depend on the beans' size and age, but 5 to 8 minutes is about right. Drain well, then return the beans to the pot.

3. Place the pot over the heat again and shake until all the water has evaporated. Transfer the beans to a warm serving bowl. Add the sesame oil, sesame seeds, coriander, and salt to taste. (Green beans need a lot of salt.) Toss well.

NOTE: Look for young slender beans such as Blue Lakes, not the wide, flat Italian types.

GREEN BEANS AND LIMAS WITH DILL

I like mixing snap beans and shell beans in quick vegetable stews with contrasting colors and textures. Flat snap beans and limas are pleasing together, but you could also pair flat snap beans and chick peas, or yellow wax beans with limas and kidney beans. Whatever the combination, these bean dishes can accompany almost anything: grilled steak, meat loaf, baked chicken, roast pork, or a salmon steak.

Serves 6

> **¾ pound green beans, preferably flat Italian snap beans, ends trimmed**
> **2 tablespoons unsalted butter**
> **½ cup minced scallions (green onions)**
> **10-ounce package frozen baby limas, thawed (see Note)**
> **3 tablespoons water or chicken stock**
> **1 tablespoon minced fresh dill**
> **Salt and freshly ground black pepper**

1. Cut the beans into 1-inch lengths. Cook them in a large pot of boiling salted water until tender, about 10 minutes. Drain them thoroughly in a sieve under cold running water to stop the cooking.

2. Melt 1½ tablespoons of butter in a large skillet over moderate heat. Add the scallions and saute until softened, about 2 minutes. Add the limas and water, stir, cover, and steam over low heat until the limas are tender, about 5 minutes. Uncover and stir in the green beans, dill, and remaining butter. Toss and season to taste with salt and pepper.

NOTE: If you are lucky enough to find fresh limas, by all means use them; just steam them with the scallions (you may need a little more liquid) until tender.

GREEN BEANS WITH PECORINO

Serve these peppery, cheese-dusted green beans with roast chicken, meat loaf, or a pork roast. I like to use the sturdy flat Romano beans for this recipe because the seasonings are so bold, but you could use any snap beans.

Serves 4 to 6

> **1 pound Romano, Kentucky Wonder, or other flat green beans, ends trimmed**
> **1 tablespoon olive oil**
> **1 cup minced onion**
> **2 cloves garlic, minced**
> **¼ to ½ teaspoon hot red pepper flakes**
> **¼ cup grated pecorino cheese**
> **Salt**

1. Blanch the beans in a large pot of heavily salted boiling water for 5 minutes; drain them under cold running water and pat them dry. Cut the beans into 1½-inch lengths.

2. Heat the oil in a large skillet over moderate heat. Add the onion, garlic, and hot pepper flakes, using the larger amount of hot pepper flakes if you like your food spicy. Saute until the onion is slightly softened, about 5 minutes. Add the beans and stir to coat them with onions. Cover, reduce the heat to low, and cook until the beans are tender, about 15 minutes. They should not need additional liquid.

3. Transfer the beans to a warm serving bowl and toss them with the cheese; taste and add salt if needed.

OTHER SERVING SUGGESTIONS

Haricots Verts

The delicate *haricots verts* should just be boiled briefly, dried, and dressed with butter or olive oil and lemon juice, salt, and pepper. They are too subtle to support much of a sauce.

Blue Lakes (or similar types)

These versatile beans can be cooked in many ways. Some of my favorites are:

WITH PESTO Toss boiled and drained beans with sliced boiled potatoes and a little pesto.

WITH DILL Reheat boiled and well-dried beans in butter with minced fresh dill.

WITH WALNUT OIL Reheat boiled and well-dried beans in butter flavored with a little walnut oil.

Kentucky Wonders and Romanos (or similar types)

Sturdy Kentucky Wonder and Romano beans take well to braising. Blanch briefly in salted water, then braise in tomato sauce seasoned with saffron, cilantro, or minced mushrooms. Or braise in bacon fat with chopped onions and garnish with crisp chopped bacon.

SUMMER VEGETABLE STEW Braise lengths of blanched flat beans with corn, zucchini, chopped tomato, and basil.

OKRA

Outside of the South, okra is little used and much maligned. When properly cooked it isn't slimy, and it tastes a good deal like green beans. In fact, like green beans, okra is delicious with Parmesan cheese or braised in tomato sauce (see page 99). When young and unblemished, okra is among the most beautiful vegetables; the slender, ridged pods, steamed and left whole, look lovely on a plate.

TO SELECT Generally, small pods are the best tasting and most tender. Choose firm, unblemished pods and handle them carefully; okra bruises easily.

TO STORE Okra is not a long keeper; it quickly gets slimy and moldy. If possible, store it in a cool, dark place and use it within a day or two; if you don't have an appropriate cool place, refrigerate it.

COOKING TIPS Whole okra pods can be steamed, boiled, braised, or deep-fried. I prefer steaming to boiling because the pods stay firmer and don't overcook as easily.

SKILLET OKRA AND PEPPERS

This is a particularly pretty dish, the green and white okra rounds flecked with bits of red pepper. Serve it with pork chops or sausages or with cornbread and black-eyed peas. A big bowl of creamy polenta would also be a nice companion. For a heartier dish, add a little more butter and a cup of raw corn kernels when you add the okra.

Serves 4

> ¾ **pound okra**
> **2 tablespoons unsalted butter**
> **1 red bell pepper, seeds and ribs removed, in neat ¼-inch dice**
> ½ **large onion, minced**
> **Pinch of hot red pepper flakes**
> **Salt**

1. Slice off and discard the tough okra stems and the skinny tips. Slice the okra crosswise into ½-inch rounds. Melt the butter in a 12-inch skillet over moderate heat. Add the bell pepper, onion, and hot pepper flakes and saute until the vegetables soften, about 10 minutes.

2. Add the okra and a large pinch of salt; stir to blend, then cover and reduce the heat so that the okra steams without burning. Check occasionally, but stir as little as possible to keep the okra from getting sticky. When the okra is tender, in about 12 to 15 minutes, taste it and add more salt if necessary. Serve in a warm serving bowl.

INDIAN-STYLE OKRA WITH TOMATOES

Niloufer Ichaporia, an accomplished Indian cook, showed me how to make a rich, complex, and easy tomato sauce without even peeling or seeding the tomatoes. She often poaches eggs on a sauce like this one, breaking the eggs right into the gently simmering liquid then covering the skillet until they're done. It makes a lovely lunch. The sauce also complements okra; the spices generate a delicious aroma and the acidity of the tomatoes appears to keep the okra from getting slimy. Don't omit the saffron; it is essential to the final flavor. It's hard to give a precise measure for saffron threads, but they are superior to saffron powder. Start with a little, then add more if you think you need it.

I could be happy with just this dish and some basmati rice for dinner, but you might want to add a broiled pork chop or a pan-fried sausage.

Serves 6

> **1 pound okra**
> **2 tablespoons vegetable oil**
> **½ teaspoon cumin seeds**
> **½ teaspoon fennel seeds**
> **½ large onion, minced**
> **2 cloves garlic, minced**
> **1-inch piece fresh ginger, peeled and very finely minced**
> **¼ teaspoon saffron threads (approximately)**
> **½ teaspoon hot red pepper flakes**
> **1 teaspoon brown sugar**
> **3½ cups coarsely chopped fresh tomatoes (no need to skin or seed)**
> **Salt**
> **2 tablespoons coarsely chopped fresh coriander (cilantro)**

1. Slice off and discard the tough okra stems and the skinny tips; slice the okra crosswise into ⅓-inch-thick rounds.

2. Heat the oil in a large skillet over moderate heat. Add the cumin and fennel seeds and saute until lightly browned and fragrant; do not allow the seeds to burn. Add the onion, garlic, and ginger and saute until softened, about 5 minutes. Add the saffron, hot pepper flakes, sugar, and tomatoes. Bring to a simmer over moderately high heat, then reduce the heat and simmer, stirring often, until the tomatoes are reduced to a thick sauce, about 20 minutes.

3. Add the okra and some salt to taste, cover the skillet, and cook until the okra is tender, about 20 to 30 minutes. Uncover and check occasionally, adding a little water if the mixture looks too dry. Stir as little as possible; stirring can cause the okra to get stringy. When the okra is tender, taste and reseason. Transfer to a serving bowl and garnish with chopped coriander.

OTHER SERVING SUGGESTIONS

STEAMED OKRA Roll steamed okra in melted butter with lemon or in the juices from a roast, or add it to a stew.

BRAISED OKRA Braise whole or sliced okra in tomato sauce. One frequent argument for cooking okra whole is that you don't release the sticky juices inside. But, as you will see if you make Indian-Style Okra with Tomatoes (page 98), sliced okra doesn't get slimy when it's cooked in tomato sauce. Perhaps the acidity of the sauce inhibits the reaction. If you are going to braise sliced okra without tomatoes (see Skillet Okra and Peppers, page 97), don't stir it too much or it will get sticky.

You can make a half-dozen variations of okra braised in tomato sauce just by varying the seasonings. Using the Indian version on page 98 as a guide, try cooking it with oregano and fresh coriander for a Mexican flavor, with basil and Parmesan cheese for Italian, or with paprika and a lot of onions for an Eastern European accent.

DEEP-FRIED OKRA Dip whole okra in any fritter batter or egg-and-crumb mixture, then deep fry.

OKRA AND CORN Okra is particularly compatible with corn. Stir sliced okra into polenta, braise it in butter with corn kernels, or add it to Corn and Limas (page 75).

PEPPERS

American cooks tend to use bell peppers as flavor accents, adding a little minced sauteed bell pepper to many vegetable and meat preparations. In Mediterranean countries, peppers are given a bigger stage. If you make the *Peperonata* on page 102 or the Grilled Peppers and Onions on page 103, you will see how enjoyable moist, meaty sweet peppers can be.

Peppers are available these days in a rainbow of colors, including red, green, yellow, orange, and purple. Most pepper varieties start out green, then change colors as they ripen. All colors will work well in the recipes in this book, although yellow, orange, red, and purple peppers generally have a sweeter, riper flavor than green ones.

"Roasted" peppers—a bit of a misnomer; actually they are broiled or grilled (see below)—improve with a few hours in a marinade. They soak up garlic, lemon juice, olive oil, and other seasonings, then generate delicious juices of their own. For that quality alone, they endear themselves to me; I'm one of those cooks who likes to have nine-tenths of a dinner made by the time company comes so I don't have to leave the table for long.

TO SELECT — Choose peppers that feel heavy for their size; they will have the thick flesh you want. Avoid peppers with soft spots or any remotely moldy smell.

TO STORE — Store unwashed peppers in a perforated plastic bag in the refrigerator; they will keep for 4 to 5 days. They do not like to be too cold; if possible, refrigerate them in the door storage area, which is the warmest part of most refrigerators.

COOKING TIPS — You don't have to cook bell peppers, of course, although I suspect most people prefer them cooked. I certainly do. You can broil or grill them whole, or they can be sliced and sauteed or braised.

Broiling To broil peppers, preheat the broiler, then arrange the peppers on the broiler pan and set it a few inches from the heat. Turn the peppers occasionally with tongs so the skin blackens and blisters all over. Transfer the peppers to a paper bag and close the bag so the peppers steam as they cool. When

100

cool, peel away the blackened skin with your fingers; do not rinse. Cut the peppers in half and remove the stem, seeds, and ribs. Cut the peeled pepper halves into pieces of the desired size.

Grilling   You can grill peppers over charcoal or over a gas grill using the same technique as in broiling. Turn the peppers over the flame until they are blackened on all sides. Cool and peel as described above.

Sauteing   Cut the peppers in half. With a small, sharp knife, cut away the stem, the seeds, and the white ribs. Slice the halves into strips of any desired width. Saute the strips in olive oil over moderate heat until tender, about 15 minutes depending on width and thickness.

Braising   Cut the peppers in half. With a small, sharp knife, cut away the stem, the seeds, and the white ribs. Slice the halves into strips of any desired width. Cook them in olive oil in a covered skillet over moderate heat until tender, about 20 minutes (depending on the width and thickness of the pieces).

PEPERONATA
(Stewed Peppers and Tomatoes, Italian Style)

Many recipes for this dish call for stewing the sliced peppers directly in the tomato sauce. It's good that way, but I find that some diners are bothered by the papery pepper skins. Here the peppers are roasted and peeled first, then marinated for several hours or overnight in a peppery tomato sauce. It's slightly more work, but you'll find it worthwhile.

Peperonata is a superb picnic dish. Enjoy it alongside or inside ham sandwiches, with grilled sausages or roast chicken, or with meaty fish such as shark, sea bass, tuna, or swordfish.

Serves 6

> 6 large, meaty bell peppers (preferably 2 red, 2 yellow, and 2 green; see Note)
> 2 tablespoons olive oil
> 1 large onion, thinly sliced
> 3 tablespoons garlic, minced
> 2 pounds ripe tomatoes, cored and cut into wedges (6 wedges each if tomatoes are small, 8 if large)
> 1½ teaspoons minced fresh oregano
> ¼ teaspoon hot red pepper flakes
> Salt
> 2 tablespoons capers
> 2 tablespoons minced parsley
> Red wine vinegar

1. Prepare a medium-hot charcoal fire or preheat the broiler. Roast the peppers, turning as necessary, until the skin is blackened all over. Put them in a closed paper bag to steam until cool. Peel them carefully (see page 100), removing all blackened bits of skin; do not rinse. Slice the peppers open and remove the stems and seeds, saving the juice if possible. Cut them into strips about ⅓ inch wide.

2. Heat the olive oil in a large heavy skillet over moderate heat. Add the onion and saute until softened, about 5 minutes. Add the garlic and saute until fragrant, about 1 minute. Add the tomatoes, cover, and cook until the tomatoes are softened, about 10 to 15 minutes. Uncover; add the oregano, hot pepper flakes, and salt to taste. Continue cooking, stirring often, until the tomato sauce is very thick and creamy, about 20 to 30 more minutes. Set aside to cool completely.

3. Stir the peppers and any juices, the capers, and parsley into the tomato sauce. Add the wine vinegar and more salt to taste. Let the peperonata stand 2 hours before serving, or cover and refrigerate it overnight and bring to room temperature before serving.

NOTE: This dish needs meaty, thick-walled peppers; look for those that seem heavy for their size.

GRILLED PEPPERS AND ONIONS

You can use any color combination of peppers in this dish—or all one color. To my taste, red bells have the sweetest, fullest flavor. The key to success is to choose thick-fleshed peppers that are heavy for their size so that you will have nicy meaty slices after roasting and peeling.

Serve at room temperature with a charcoal-grilled steak, sausages, or burgers; with grilled rock cod or swordfish; or with a garlicky roast chicken. Prepare the peppers and onions first, then restoke the grill with coals for your meat.

Serves 6

> ¼ cup extra virgin olive oil, plus more for brushing
> 2 cloves garlic, minced
> 2 tablespoons red wine vinegar, or more to taste
> Salt
> 2 red bell peppers
> 2 yellow bell peppers
> 2 green bell peppers
> 1 large yellow onion
> ¼ cup minced parsley
> 1 tablespoon minced fresh mint, or more to taste

1. Prepare a hot charcoal fire. While you're waiting for the fire, heat ¼ cup of olive oil in a small skillet over low heat. Add the garlic and saute until fragrant, about 1 minute. Remove from the heat and transfer the garlic and oil to a large bowl; let them cool, then whisk in 2 tablespoons of vinegar and salt to taste. Set aside.

2. Grill the peppers over the charcoal, turning them as each side blisters and blackens.

When blackened on all sides, put the peppers in a paper bag and close the bag to allow the peppers to steam.

3. Halve the onion through the root end but do not peel it. Brush the cut side of the onion halves with olive oil, then grill them cut side down over the hot part of the fire until they are lightly charred. Turn them cut side up and move them to a cooler part of the fire where they will cook by indirect heat. Cover the grill, leaving the vents open, and continue cooking the onions until they are softened, about 30 minutes. Remove them from the heat; when cool enough to handle, trim away the root and stem ends and peel away the outer layers of skin. Cut the halves from stem to root end into slices about ¼ inch thick. Put the slices in the bowl with the vinaigrette.

4. Peel the peppers (see page 100), carefully removing all seeds and ribs; slice the peppers into ½-inch strips. Add them to the bowl; toss to blend. Set the bowl aside for 30 minutes to allow the flavor to develop, then add the parsley and 1 tablespoon of mint; toss. Taste and adjust the seasoning.

OTHER SERVING SUGGESTIONS

SAUTEED PEPPERS AND ONIONS Saute sliced onions, sliced peppers, and minced garlic in a little olive oil until the peppers are tender.

PEPPERS AND POTATOES Dice some red, yellow, and green peppers. Saute them in bacon fat until tender, then add some sliced or cubed boiled potatoes and parsley and toss to heat through.

SUMMER SAUTE Peppers are compatible with other summer vegetables like zucchini, tomatoes, and corn. One possibility: saute some diced peppers until tender, then stir in raw corn kernels, diced zucchini, and some finely minced ham. Cover and cook until the corn and zucchini are just tender.

SUMMER SQUASH

Zucchini (both green and golden), yellow crookneck squash, and the small rounded pattypan and scallopini squashes qualify as summer squashes because of their thin edible skins. Summer squash is almost a misnomer now that Mexico and other warm growing areas keep these thin-skinned squashes in the markets almost year-round. Nevertheless, in most parts of this country they are a summer vegetable, and you will be most likely to find a plentiful supply from local sources in summer.

Summer squash have a high water content and are easy to cook to mush. I should know: my dear mother did it regularly. That's why I grew up thinking that squash was watery and bland, a vegetable to layer in a casserole with lots of butter, eggs, cracker crumbs, and cheese. When you do taste young, firm squash that hasn't been overcooked, you recognize that it has its own distinctive, cucumber-like flavor.

Crookneck squash are sweeter than zucchini but seedier. Zucchini are worth eating only when they are young and slender; otherwise, they are watery and bitter. The pale green pattypan and deep green scallopini squashes have the taste and dense texture of young zucchini. With their turban shapes, they lend themselves best to being cut into wedges.

TO SELECT
For best flavor, choose small to medium squash with no soft spots; large squash are usually seedy and watery.

TO STORE
Summer squash do not like to be too cold. Refrigerate in a perforated plastic bag in the warmest part of the refrigerator, such as a door storage area, and use within 2 to 3 days. Wash just before using.

COOKING TIPS
Summer squash can be steamed, sauteed, baked, broiled, grilled, or deep-fried.

Quick Cooking For quick cooking, grate summer squash coarsely in a food processor or with a four-sided grater. Salt the grated squash, then let it stand in a sieve or colander 30 minutes to drain. Rinse under cold running water, then squeeze in a clean dish towel to remove excess moisture. Saute in butter or olive oil until the squash just loses its rawness, adding minced garlic at the beginning and minced parsley at the end.

BROILED ZUCCHINI WITH BUTTER AND PARMESAN

The success of this simple recipe depends on using small, firm-fleshed zucchini, not the large, seedy, watery ones. Zucchini that are about 5 to 6 inches long and ¾ to 1 inch in diameter are what I call "medium" and are about as big as you should go. One medium zucchini, halved, makes a single portion. If you can find firm, fresh smaller ones, so much the better.

Serve with roast or grilled beef, meat loaf, or baked chicken. A meat dish with a tomato component—braised beef in tomato sauce, for example—would be a particularly happy match.

Serves 4

> **4 medium or 6 small zucchini**
> **1½ tablespoons melted butter**
> **Salt and freshly ground black pepper**
> **½ cup grated Parmesan cheese**

1. Bring about an inch of salted water to a boil in the bottom of a steamer. Scrub the zucchini and put them, whole, in the top of the steamer. Steam until just tender; cooking time will depend on size, but 10 minutes should be about right. They should give to the touch, but remember that they will continue to cook as they cool; be careful not to overcook them. Let them cool, then halve them lengthwise, leaving the stem ends attached.

2. Preheat the broiler. Put the butter in the bottom of a low-sided baking dish just large enough to hold the zucchini halves in one layer. Put the zucchini in the dish cut side down, then turn them cut side up to coat them with butter. Season with salt and pepper. Sprinkle with the cheese. Broil until golden brown, watching carefully. Serve immediately.

JEANNE'S SUMMER SQUASH

My friend Jeanne Quan brought these beautiful feta-stuffed squash to a birthday party and we grilled them alongside some skirt steaks. You can stuff them several hours ahead as Jeanne did, but they should be grilled just before serving. Depending on the size of the squash and their seed cavities, you may not need all the feta cheese, but buy at least ⅓ pound to be safe. Any extra filling will be delicious spread on a cracker or in a celery rib for a pre-dinner nibble.

Serves 4 to 6

> **6 scallopini or pattypan squash (about 1¼ pounds)**
> **⅓ pound imported feta cheese**
> **2 teaspoons minced fresh dill**
> **Freshly ground black pepper**
> **2 tablespoons olive oil (approximately), plus more for brushing**

1. Trim off the stem ends of the squash; cut each squash in half horizontally. Carefully hollow out the seed cavities with a spoon or melon baller, taking care not to pierce the squash all the way through.

2. Combine the feta, dill, several grinds of black pepper, and enough olive oil to make a creamy spread; the amount of oil will depend on the creaminess of your feta. Blend with a wooden spoon until fairly smooth.

3. Brush the squash halves all over with olive oil. Fill the seed cavities with the cheese mixture, mounding it slightly. Each half will probably take at least ½ tablespoon of filling.

4. Prepare a medium charcoal fire. Grill the squash halves stuffing side up on a cool part of the fire until they are tender. Depending on the heat of the grill and the thickness of your squash, this may take 20 to 25 minutes. Don't cook the squash too fast or they will burn before they soften. When the squash are just tender, transfer them with a spatula to a warm serving platter. Serve immediately.

OTHER SERVING SUGGESTIONS

STEAMED SQUASH WITH ONION Steam chunks of summer squash with chunks of onion, then dress them with slivers of butter, salt, paprika, and parsley. Try other herbs as well: fresh dill, chives, chervil, tarragon, and coriander (cilantro) all complement summer squash.

TOMATOES

Sometimes when I walk into the market in late summer I can smell the tomatoes the moment I hit the door. When that happens, it doesn't matter what I had planned to buy for dinner—we're having tomatoes. To my taste, a ripe tomato is the world's most seductive vegetable. For the few weeks in summer when I can get local vine-ripened tomatoes, I use them constantly.

TO SELECT

Tomatoes should smell like tomatoes. If they have no aroma, put them back. Don't be fooled by a beautiful even red color; fragrance is the key to a good tomato. Ripe tomatoes are fragile, which is why tomatoes that must be shipped long distances are picked underripe. To find the best tomatoes, shop at farmers' markets or at retail markets that buy from local growers. Get your fill when local tomatoes are in season, then put your tomato recipes aside until next year.

Tomato varieties can be loosely divided into two camps: salad tomatoes and sauce tomatoes. Salad tomatoes can be as tiny as grapes or as large as the famous "beefsteak" varieties. When ripe, they may be yellow, orange, red, or even green. If a tomato is delicious and juicy when raw, consider it a salad tomato.

Sauce tomatoes are bred to have proportionally more pulp and less juice. They cook down quickly into a thick puree. The familiar plum-shaped Roma tomato is a sauce tomato, as is anything else labeled plum tomato or paste tomato in the market. In my own kitchen, I'm pretty flexible. I never use sauce tomatoes for salad, but I do frequently use salad tomatoes for sauce because they are often better tasting than commercial sauce tomatoes. Just bear in mind that salad tomatoes have more seeds and more juice and will take a while to cook down into a sauce; you can remove the skin, seeds, and juice if you like (see page 109), but I rarely do.

TO STORE

Never refrigerate tomatoes unless they are threatening to become overripe. Store ripe tomatoes at cool room temperature (65° to 70°) away from direct sunlight and use them within 3 to 4 days. If you can, put them on a rack with some space between them to allow for air circulation. Ripen green or partially red tomatoes in a dark place at cool room temperature. Pack them in one or two layers in shallow boxes or on trays or, if you have just a few, keep them in a paper bag. A closed container will trap some of the tomatoes' natural ethylene gas and accelerate ripening. However, they will not taste as good as vine-ripened tomatoes. Despite the common practice, it is not a good idea to ripen tomatoes on a window sill; they can quickly get too hot.

PREPARATION
TIPS

To peel and seed tomatoes, peel the tomatoes first; then core them with a small, sharp knife; then remove the seeds and juice.

Peeling To peel a tomato, cut an "X" on the bottom. Blanch the tomato for 30 seconds in boiling water, then transfer it with a slotted spoon to a bowl of ice water. When cool, lift it out of the water and peel the skin back from the "X." It will slip off easily.

Seeding To seed a tomato, cut it in half horizontally. Holding one half upside-down over a bowl or the sink, use the fingers of the other hand to pry the seeds and juice loose.

BAKED TOMATOES WITH FETA

This is an extremely simple recipe and one you can make all summer long without tiring of it. Vary it by replacing the feta topping with a swipe of pesto (page 116) or storebought tapenade (olive paste). Serve these soft, juicy tomatoes with grilled lamb chops, leg of lamb, or grilled fish or shrimp. Leftover tomatoes are delicious as a sandwich the next day, between two slices of good toasted bread.

Serves 4

> **4 large ripe tomatoes**
> **2 tablespoons olive oil**
> **Salt and freshly ground black pepper**
> **1 teaspoon minced fresh oregano**
> **⅓ pound imported feta cheese, in one piece**
> **1 tablespoon minced parsley**

1. Preheat the oven to 325°. Core the tomatoes and slice off about ⅓ inch from the stem end of each to make a flat surface. Put the olive oil in a baking dish just large enough to hold the tomatoes. Set the tomatoes in the dish cut side down. Bake 45 minutes.

2. Using a spatula, turn the tomatoes cut side up. Spoon the pan juices over them and season them with salt, pepper, and oregano. Continue baking until they are soft but not mushy, about 30 to 45 minutes. Transfer the tomatoes to a warm serving platter or individual dinner plates. Pour the pan juices over them. Grate the cheese thickly on top and garnish with minced parsley.

TOMATO BREAD CRISP

Please save this dish for those few weeks in summer when you can get sweet, dead-ripe, full-flavored tomatoes. And please don't serve it hot; it is best at room temperature. I like to mix Parmesan and pecorino cheeses—the former has a nutty flavor, the latter a sharp one—but you can use all one or the other, if you prefer.

Serves 6

> 3 cups fine fresh breadcrumbs
> ¼ cup minced parsley
> ¼ cup freshly grated Parmesan cheese
> ¼ cup freshly grated pecorino cheese
> 1 clove garlic, minced
> 5 tablespoons olive oil
> Salt and freshly ground black pepper
> 2 pounds vine-ripe tomatoes

1. Preheat the oven to 375°. Spread the breadcrumbs on a baking sheet and toast them in the oven for 10 minutes; they should be dry and lightly colored but not browned. Combine them in a bowl with the parsley, Parmesan, pecorino, garlic, and olive oil. Toss well with a fork to blend. Season highly with salt and pepper.

2. Cut a skin-deep "X" in the bottom of each tomato. Bring a large pot of water to a boil over high heat. Add the tomatoes and simmer for 30 seconds, then lift them out with a slotted spoon and plunge them into a bowl of ice water. When they are cool, the skin should peel back easily from the "X." Core the tomatoes and slice them ¼ inch thick.

3. Put one-third of the breadcrumb mixture in the bottom of a gratin dish, approximately 14 by 8 by 2 inches. Top with half the sliced tomatoes. Top with another third of the breadcrumbs, then with the remaining tomatoes, then with the remaining breadcrumbs. Bake until browned and crisp, about 55 minutes. Let cool to room temperature before serving.

SLICED TOMATOES WITH BUTTERMILK DRESSING

I particularly like the way this creamy, herby dressing mingles with sliced tomato juices; be sure to have some sturdy bread for dipping. The dressing is good for other salads too. Try it on shredded cabbage for cole slaw, with sliced beets or cucumbers, or with hearts of romaine. This salad would complement a grilled or broiled sirloin steak or a juicy hamburger steak.

Serves 4

> ½ cup mayonnaise or sour cream
> ½ cup buttermilk
> 1½ tablespoons minced fresh dill
> 3 tablespoons minced scallions (green onions)
> 1 clove garlic, minced
> Salt and freshly ground black pepper
> 3 large or 4 small vine-ripe tomatoes
> Red wine vinegar

1. Whisk together the mayonnaise, buttermilk, dill, scallions, garlic, and salt and pepper to taste. Set aside for half an hour to blend flavors.

2. Slice the tomatoes to the desired thickness and arrange them on a serving platter. Sprinkle with salt and vinegar. Drizzle with buttermilk dressing.

PANZANELLA
(Tuscan Bread Salad)

This juicy salad is just one example of the Italian genius for using leftover bread. In Tuscany, the source of this recipe, cooks use a dense, country-style loaf. Look for something similar, a dense French- or Italian-style unsliced bread containing only flour, water, yeast, and salt. It should be a large loaf, not a baguette, and it should be at least a day old. If it still feels somewhat fresh, wait another day; fresh (or airy-textured) bread won't hold up in the vinaigrette.

Don't make this salad unless you can get height-of-summer, vine-ripened tomatoes. Their flavor is essential to good results.

Panzanella is particularly good with charcoal-grilled meat or fish. Try it with grilled swordfish, tuna, sausages, or flank steak.

113

Serves 6

½ small red onion, thinly sliced
6 ounces stale bread, crust removed (see introduction)
4 tablespoons olive oil
3 large ripe tomatoes, peeled, seeded, and cut into ½-inch dice
¾ cup thinly sliced celery heart (pale part only)
½ English cucumber, peeled, seeded, and cut into ½-inch dice
12 leaves fresh basil, julienned
2 teaspoons minced garlic
2 tablespoons capers, coarsely chopped
1 to 1½ tablespoons red wine vinegar
Salt and freshly ground black pepper

1. Unless the onion is sweet, soak the slices in cold water for 30 minutes, changing the water several times, to draw out the hotness. Drain and pat dry.

2. Preheat the oven to 400°. Cut the bread into ¾-inch cubes. Heat 2 tablespoons of the oil in a large, heavy skillet over moderately high heat. Add the bread cubes and toss to coat them with oil; if your skillet isn't large enough to hold all the bread cubes comfortably, do this in two batches, using 1 tablespoon of oil each time. Transfer the bread cubes to a baking sheet and bake until lightly browned and crisp, about 10 to 15 minutes. Set aside to cool.

3. In a large bowl combine the tomatoes, onion, celery, cucumber, basil, garlic, capers, 1 tablespoon wine vinegar, and the remaining 2 tablespoons of olive oil. Toss to blend. Season to taste with salt and pepper. Add the bread cubes, toss again, taste, and adjust the seasoning, adding more vinegar if desired. Serve immediately.

TOMATOES WITH ARUGULA PESTO

Purists will say that pesto can be made only with basil; I'm bending that definition a little. This pungent pesto is made with nutty arugula (also known as roquette). Slathered on juicy sliced tomatoes, it makes a quick summer dish to serve with grilled chicken or swordfish steaks. For the unconvinced, I have included a recipe for traditional pesto (see Variation).

Serves 4 (see Note)

> ½ cup walnuts
> 2 cups coarsely chopped arugula leaves, stems removed (see Note)
> 2 cloves garlic
> ⅞ cup olive oil
> ½ cup grated Parmesan cheese
> Salt and freshly ground black pepper
> 3 large vine-ripened tomatoes
> Red or white wine vinegar

1. Preheat the oven to 325°. Toast the walnuts on a cookie sheet until fragrant, about 15 minutes; let them cool. Put the arugula leaves in a food processor. Peel the garlic, slice it into thin slivers, and add it. Process until almost smooth, stopping the machine to scrape down the sides of the bowl once or twice. Add the walnuts and process until almost smooth. With the machine running, add the olive oil through the feed tube in a slow stream. Transfer the mixture to a bowl and stir in the cheese by hand. Season to taste with salt and pepper. You will have about 1⅓ cups of pesto.

2. Slice the tomatoes as thick as you like. Arrange the slices on a platter, salt them to taste, and sprinkle them with wine vinegar. Spread a little pesto on each slice. Serve immediately. Be sure to provide good crusty bread for soaking up the juices.

VARIATION: To make a traditional pesto, substitute pine nuts for the walnuts; toast them in a small dry skillet over low heat, shaking the skillet often, until lightly colored. In place of the arugula use 2 cups of coarsely chopped basil leaves (firmly packed). Increase the Parmesan cheese to ¾ cup.

NOTE: This recipe makes more pesto than you'll need. Freeze the rest with a thin film of oil on top to prevent it from oxidizing, or refrigerate it and use it over the next few days as a sandwich spread, a topping for vegetable soup, or a pasta sauce.

NOTE: If possible, taste the arugula before buying it. The leaves should be nutty and just slightly peppery, not bitter or hot. The pesto isn't worth making if the leaves are hot. Small, young leaves are generally the best tasting.

OTHER SERVING SUGGESTIONS

For ease of preparation and flavor, no side dish can beat ripe sliced tomatoes. A platter of sliced tomatoes is the ideal summer partner to grilled fish, fowl, and red meat of all kinds. Here are some of the ways I like to serve them:

TOMATO AND ONION SALAD Layer tomato slices with paper-thin rings of red onion. (If the onions taste hot, soak them for an hour in several changes of cold water.) Drizzle with vinaigrette, then scatter some sliced *peperoncini* (mild Italian peppers) and minced Italian parsley on top.

TOMATO SALAD WITH FRESH MAYONNAISE Top sliced tomatoes with fresh homemade mayonnaise seasoned with minced shallots, capers, anchovy paste, and tarragon.

TOMATO SALAD WITH FRESH HERBS Make a mixture of minced herbs—parsley, chives, chervil, tarragon—and sprinkle it generously over sliced tomatoes. Drizzle with vinaigrette.

SLICED TOMATOES WITH GUACAMOLE Top sliced tomatoes with a dollop of guacamole—coarsely mashed avocado seasoned to taste with minced green chile and onion, salt, lime juice, and fresh coriander (cilantro).

AUTUMN

BRUSSELS SPROUTS	Brussels Sprouts, Pearl Onions, and Mushrooms
	Brussels Sprouts with Walnut Oil
HARD-SHELLED SQUASH	Roast Autumn Squash with Cardamom Butter
	Autumn Squash and Parsnip Puree
	Autumn Squash and Corn
JERUSALEM ARTICHOKES	Roast Jerusalem Artichokes with Garlic and Thyme
	Jerusalem Artichokes and Peas
SWEET POTATOES	Rutabaga-Sweet Potato Puree
	Sweet Potatoes, Parsnips, and Peas

AUTUMN HAS ARRIVED when the bright yellows, greens, and reds of the summer produce market give way to forest greens, earthy browns, and rich gold and copper tones. Cooler weather brings cooler colors and a heightened appetite for richer dishes; vegetable purees and vegetable stews suddenly have more appeal.

In autumn I turn from grilling to cooking more roasts and stews, which present opportunities for some easy side dishes. I might tuck peeled and quartered sweet potatoes or acorn squash wedges around a pork roast or arrange whole, scrubbed Jerusalem artichokes around a beef pot roast. I like blanched and halved brussels sprouts added to a pork stew or reheated in the deglazed drippings from a roast chicken (see page 125).

The autumn produce market can seem a little thin after the summer vegetables vanish and before the winter crops arrive. During those few weeks, you can add variety with year-round vegetables such as cauliflower, potatoes, carrots, and mushrooms. In any case, produce seasons are invariably weather-dependent. In some years, high-quality "summer" tomatoes and peppers are available well into autumn, or winter root vegetables show up early. When that happens, both summer and winter produce can make delicious autumn eating.

BRUSSELS SPROUTS

I enjoy brussels sprouts but can understand why these miniature members of the cabbage family have some passionate foes. If they're old and overgrown or overcooked, they can be nasty. But small, fresh, mild-tasting sprouts, carefully cooked, are a treat. They require so little preparation and cook so quickly that I make them often for autumn meals.

TO SELECT   Freshness and youth are important. Choose small, compact sprouts with no sign of yellowing. They should smell mild and sweet, not strong.

TO STORE   Refrigerate in the vegetable crisper in a perforated plastic bag and use within a day or two.

COOKING TIPS   Wash sprouts well and pat them dry. Trim the butt end of each to remove any rough, brown parts, but don't trim too much or the leaves will come off. Cut an "X" into the butt end to help the sprouts cook quickly.

Brussels sprouts can be steamed or boiled. (See Broccoli, page 145, for a discussion of the pros and cons of both methods.) I prefer to boil them, but the choice is yours. Whether steaming or boiling, if you are not going to eat them right away, "shock" them under cold running water to stop the cooking, then pat them dry.

BRUSSELS SPROUTS, PEARL ONIONS, AND MUSHROOMS

Brussels sprouts and mushrooms braised in butter with no added liquid turn an appetizing golden brown. Toss them with glazed pearl onions to make a side dish that would complement turkey, ham, or game.

Serves 4

> **16 pearl onions, about ¾ to 1 inch in diameter**
> **2 tablespoons butter**
> **½ cup chicken stock**
> **½ pound brussels sprouts**
> **½ pound mushrooms**
> **Salt and freshly ground black pepper**
> **1½ tablespoons minced fresh dill, parsley, or mint (optional)**

1. To peel the onions easily, bring a small pot of water to a boil. Add the onions and boil 1 minute, then drain. Peel while hot. Trim the root end of each onion but not too much or the onions will come apart in cooking.

2. Melt ½ tablespoon of butter in a small lidded skillet over moderate heat; add the onions and chicken stock. Cover, reduce the heat, and simmer until the onions are tender and lightly browned in spots and the chicken stock has reduced to a glaze. Watch carefully and lower the heat if the stock threatens to reduce too much before the onions are tender. Set aside.

3. Trim the ends of the brussels sprouts and cut them in half. Clean the mushrooms with a damp cloth and trim the ends; halve the mushrooms. Melt the remaining butter in a heavy 10-inch skillet over moderately high heat. Add the brussels sprouts and mushrooms. Season generously with salt and pepper. Cook briskly, uncovered, shaking the pan occasionally, until the mushrooms and sprouts are nicely browned, about 12 to 15 minutes. Reduce the heat as necessary to allow the vegetables to cook through without over-browning, but do not add any liquid; the sprouts will cook in the steam given off by the mushrooms.

4. When the vegetables are appetizingly colored and fully cooked, add the onions and any juices in the skillet, toss, and heat through. Transfer to a warm serving bowl, add minced herbs if desired, and toss to coat.

BRUSSELS SPROUTS WITH WALNUT OIL

A lot of cooks pair brussels sprouts and toasted nuts; I prefer this more subtle preparation. Try it with roast chicken, roast duck, or game. I can also imagine these sprouts making a pretty pile in the center of a crown roast of pork. Please reserve this simple recipe for a time when you can find small brussels sprouts that are sure to be mild.

Serves 4

> **12 ounces brussels sprouts**
> **2 teaspoons unsalted butter**
> **2 teaspoons walnut oil**
> **1 tablespoon minced parsley**
> **Salt and freshly ground black pepper**

1. Trim off any darkened areas on the base of each sprout. Cut an "X" in the base, about ¼ inch deep, to help the sprouts to cook through quickly.

2. Bring a large pot of salted water to a boil over high heat. Add the sprouts and cook until just tender, about 7 to 10 minutes. Drain the sprouts in a sieve, then return them to the pot and set it over moderate heat. Shake the pot until all the water has evaporated.

3. Put the sprouts in a warm serving bowl. Add the butter, oil, parsley, and salt and pepper to taste. Toss to coat the sprouts evenly with the seasonings.

OTHER SERVING SUGGESTIONS

BRUSSELS SPROUTS IN CREAM Slice partially cooked brussels sprouts thinly or cut them into quarters or halves. Reheat them in enough butter to coat, then add cream and simmer until it is reduced and thick. Season with nutmeg.

BRUSSELS SPROUTS WITH GINGER Toss cooked sprouts in butter seasoned with grated fresh ginger.

BRUSSELS SPROUTS WITH BACON Render some chopped bacon or Italian pancetta (unsmoked bacon); pour off the excess fat. Add cooked brussels sprouts and toss to reheat.

BRUSSELS SPROUTS WITH TOASTED NUTS Slice cooked brussels sprouts thinly or cut them into quarters. Reheat them in butter; add toasted pine nuts, slivered almonds, or pecans just before serving.

BRUSSELS SPROUTS IN PAN JUICES I like blanched and halved brussels sprouts reheated in the deglazed drippings from a roast chicken. When the chicken is done, pour any fat out of the roasting pan, add about ½ cup dry white wine, and put the pan over high heat. Cook, scraping up the drippings with a wooden spoon, until the liquid has reduced by about half and the drippings have dissolved and created a light sauce. Reheat the sprouts in enough of the sauce to coat them lightly.

HARD-SHELLED SQUASH

This category includes butternut, kabocha, acorn, buttercup, delicata, mini pumpkin, sweet dumpling, turban, and dozens of other squashes. I usually call them winter squashes but that's not strictly accurate since most of them start showing up in the markets in autumn. What distinguishes them from zucchini, pattypan, crookneck, and other "summer squashes" is their hard shell, which makes them excellent keepers.

I particularly like butternut, the elongated, smooth-skinned, buff-colored squash with one bulbous end. Its meat is firm and sweet but not sugary, and its shell is not so hard that you need a major-league cleaver to cut it. Its smooth, unfurrowed shell is also relatively easy to peel.

The kabocha squashes are also favorites, although it takes a cleaver to cut them. Kabocha is the generic name for several varieties of Japanese squash; all have sweet, firm flesh.

Also consider the small, dark green acorn squash; half a baked acorn squash makes an attractive serving.

TO SELECT

Specialty produce markets and even some supermarkets carry a wide variety of hard-shelled squashes these days. They vary almost as much in the firmness and sweetness of their flesh as they do in appearance. It will take some experimenting to know which varieties you like best.

Hard squashes are such good keepers that you're unlikely to have trouble finding a good one. They shouldn't have any soft spots, moldy spots, or significant blemishes, and the stem should be intact. If the squash has been cut into pieces, the pieces should not look dried out.

TO STORE

Store in a cool place. Most varieties, uncut, will keep for at least a month. After cutting, wrap any unused portion in plastic wrap, refrigerate, and use within 3 or 4 days.

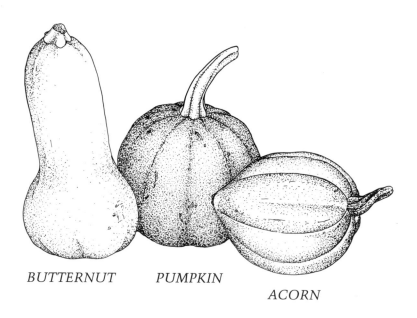

BUTTERNUT   *PUMPKIN*

ACORN

126

COOKING TIPS   Please be careful cutting open these squashes. Some of them have very hard, thick skins and you need a large, heavy knife—preferably a Chinese cleaver—to cut them open. If you don't know how you're going to get it open once you get it home, buy precut squash.

Peeling   Hard-shelled squash can be cooked and served in the skin—no need to peel. For purees, bake or steam the squash in the skin first; you can then easily scoop the cooked flesh away from the skin with a spoon (see Autumn Squash and Parsnip Puree, page 129). For dishes that require peeled raw squash, choose a relatively thin-skinned variety such as butternut or delicata squash.

Baking   I think baking or steaming is best for these squashes. To bake, cut the unpeeled squash into serving-size pieces, remove any seeds and strings, arrange the pieces in a buttered baking dish, season, cover, and bake in a 350° oven until tender.

Steaming   Cook unpeeled squash halves or wedges in a covered steamer until tender. Season with butter, salt, and pepper.

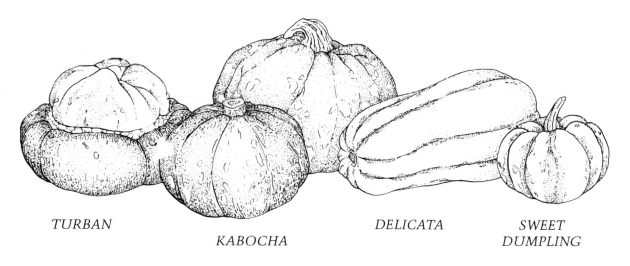

TURBAN

KABOCHA

DELICATA

*SWEET
DUMPLING*

ROAST AUTUMN SQUASH WITH CARDAMOM BUTTER

Because this is such a simple recipe, the ingredients have to be absolutely right. The squash must be a sweet one, such as a kabocha or the dark green buttercup. If you are unsure, ask the produce manager to point out the sweetest hard-shelled squashes. Also, this dish will be best if you buy cardamom pods and use a mortar and pestle to pound the seeds yourself. If you don't have a mortar and pestle, make sure your ground cardamom smells fresh and pungent; replace it if it doesn't.

I like the sweetness of hard-shelled squash with pork, but these buttery wedges would also complement roast duck, goose, turkey, venison, or other full-flavored game.

Serves 4

> **1 sweet hard-shelled squash, 3 to 3½ pounds**
> *or* **4 wedges hard-shelled squash (skin on), about 12 ounces each**
> **2 tablespoons unsalted butter, softened, plus more for the baking dish**
> **Salt**
> **¼ teaspoon freshly ground cardamom**

1. Preheat the oven to 350°. If your squash is whole, carefully cut it in half (a Chinese cleaver is best for this) and remove all the seeds and strings. Cut each half into 2 equal wedges; they should be about 12 ounces each.

2. Place the wedges in a lightly buttered baking dish. Salt them lightly. Cover the dish with a lid or aluminum foil and bake until the squash is tender, about 45 minutes.

3. While the squash is baking, combine the softened butter and cardamom in a small bowl. Season to taste with salt.

4. Transfer the squash wedges to individual plates. Spoon any buttery pan juices over them. Put a spoonful of cardamom butter in each cavity.

AUTUMN SQUASH AND PARSNIP PUREE

Autumn squash purees are too sweet for my taste; I like to cut the sweetness with parsnips, which add a subtle nutty flavor. The two together make a distinctive puree that is better than the sum of its parts. Try it with the Thanksgiving turkey, a holiday ham, roast pork loin, roast duck, or quail.

Serves 4 to 6

> **1 pound sweet hard-skinned squash, such as butternut**
> **¾ pound parsnips**
> **2 tablespoons butter**
> **Salt and freshly ground black pepper**
> **Freshly grated nutmeg**

1. Preheat oven to 375°. If your squash is whole, cut it open; remove the seeds and strings. Cut the squash into eight equal pieces. Arrange the pieces in one layer in a lightly oiled baking dish. Cover the dish tightly with a lid or aluminum foil and bake until the squash is tender, about 45 minutes. Set aside to cool slightly.

2. Peel the parsnips, discarding the ends. Cut the flesh into ½-inch pieces. Place the pieces in a 3-quart saucepan with ½ cup of lightly salted water. Bring it to a simmer over high heat, cover, and reduce the heat. Simmer until the parsnips are tender, about 10 minutes. Lower the heat as necessary to keep all the water from evaporating; if necessary add a little more water, but the water should have completely evaporated by the time the parsnips are done.

3. Put the parsnips in a food processor fitted with a steel blade. Using a large spoon, scrape in the squash flesh; discard the skins. Puree until smooth. Transfer the puree to a clean saucepan. Cut the butter into small pieces and add them; reheat the puree over low heat, stirring. Season to taste with salt, pepper, and nutmeg.

AUTUMN SQUASH AND CORN

These two all-American vegetables are delicious together. Take advantage of their compatibility during that brief time in early autumn when the last of the sweet corn and the first of the autumn squash are in the markets at the same time. I prefer butternut squash for this recipe because it is exceptionally sweet and it's easy to peel when raw. Roast chicken, pork chops, or a braised pork shoulder would be good companions.

Serves 4

> **1½ tablespoons butter**
> **⅓ cup minced red bell pepper**
> **12 ounces peeled hard-shelled squash, in ½-inch cubes**
> **2 cups fresh corn kernels**
> **Salt and freshly ground black pepper**

Melt the butter in a heavy, 10-inch skillet over moderate heat. Add the bell pepper and saute until it is slightly softened, about 5 minutes. Add the squash and corn and toss to coat them with butter. Cover the skillet, reduce the heat to low, and cook until the squash and corn are tender, about 10 to 15 minutes. Shake the pan occasionally to keep the squash from sticking (lift the cover a few times to check). Season to taste with salt and pepper before serving.

OTHER SERVING SUGGESTIONS

ROASTED SQUASH Arrange 1½- to 2-inch chunks of peeled butternut squash around a pot roast about 30 minutes before the roast is done; cover and continue baking until the squash is tender.

SAUTEED SQUASH Saute peeled and sliced, diced, or grated squash in butter; cover the skillet to steam the squash until done (see Autumn Squash and Corn, page 130).

SQUASH PUREES Some of the firm-textured squashes like kabocha and butternut make good purees. Bake wedges first, in the skin, then scoop out the flesh and puree it with butter, salt, pepper, and a little nutmeg or mace.

Autumn Squash and Corn

JERUSALEM ARTICHOKES

These knobby tubers are unrelated to artichokes and have nothing to do with Jerusalem. They are members of the sunflower family, which may explain why they are sometimes called "sunchokes." The Jerusalem connection may come from the French and Italian word for sunflower: *girasole*.

To my palate, Jerusalem artichokes taste like a cross of celery root and potato, with perhaps a little artichoke mixed in. The flavor is delicious but hard to describe, which is why you ought to taste these sweet, crunchy tubers for yourself.

Fresh-picked Jerusalem artichokes are mostly carbohydrate, but a type of carbohydrate (inulin) that isn't used by the body. Therefore, they are quite low in calories—about 7 calories per 3½ ounces. During storage, the calorie count rises as the inulin converts to simple sugars, but even at the maximum, they provide only about 75 calories per 3½ ounces.

TO SELECT

Jerusalem artichokes should be firm, with no sign of shriveling. For even cooking and easy peeling, try to find tubers of approximately the same thickness and without a lot of crevices or knobby parts.

TO STORE

Store in a perforated plastic bag in your refrigerator crisper. They will keep for about a week.

COOKING TIPS

However you cook Jerusalem artichokes, take care not to overcook them; they should still have a hint of crunchiness to them. Check them often because they quickly go from firm to mushy. The thin skin is edible but you can peel it if you prefer. Peeled chokes oxidize quickly; to prevent them from browning, put them in water acidulated with lemon juice until you're ready to cook them.

Baking The easiest and perhaps the best way to cook Jerusalem artichokes is to bake them. First scrub them well, making sure you get any dirt out of the crevices; then roll them in butter or oil and bake them uncovered in a 350° oven until tender. Or you can bake them in a covered dish with aromatic ingredients, as in Roast Jerusalem Artichokes with Garlic and Thyme (page 134).

Sauteing Grate or slice Jerusalem artichokes—peeled or un-peeled—before sauteing them in butter.

Braising Dice Jerusalem artichokes and braise them with other vegetables, as in Jerusalem Artichokes with Peas (page 135). Other compatible braising partners include carrots, broccoli stems, or turnip greens.

Steaming You can boil Jerusalem artichokes, but I think they tend to get waterlogged that way. Instead, steam them whole over boiling salted water, then slice them and dot with butter.

ROAST JERUSALEM ARTICHOKES WITH GARLIC AND THYME

Roast Jerusalem artichokes whole in a covered, buttered baking dish and you won't quite believe what happens. They generate their own delicious "sauce"—reduced, almost caramelized juices that taste something like meat glaze. Slice them thickly after baking and spoon the glaze over them to make an unusual dish to accompany steak or a pork roast. Jerusalem artichokes are naturally low in calories, and this preparation doesn't add many more.

Serves 4

> **1 pound Jerusalem artichokes (see Note)**
> **1 tablespoon unsalted butter**
> **Salt and freshly ground black pepper**
> **½ teaspoon minced fresh thyme**
> **2 whole cloves garlic, unpeeled**

1. Preheat the oven to 375°. Scrub the Jerusalem artichokes with a clean pot scrubber or other coarse brush to remove any dirt. Scrubbing will remove some of the skin, which is fine, but you don't need to remove all the skin.

2. Use the butter to generously grease the bottom and sides of a covered baking dish just large enough to hold the artichokes (they don't have to be in one layer). Put the artichokes in the dish, season them with salt and pepper, and scatter thyme and garlic cloves in the dish. Cover and bake until the artichokes are just tender and still crisp. Cooking time will depend on size, but start checking after 30 minutes by piercing them with a small sharp knife. Don't let them get soft.

3. When the artichokes are done, transfer them to a cutting board and cut them into ¼-inch-thick slices. Arrange the slices on a warm serving platter. There will be some wonderful glaze-like juices in the bottom of the baking dish; spoon them over the slices. Use a rubber spatula if necessary to get all the juices and spread them on the artichokes. A garlic-loving guest may enjoy the garlic cloves.

NOTE: Try to buy Jerusalem artichokes of approximately equal size so that they cook evenly.

JERUSALEM ARTICHOKES AND PEAS

During late fall and winter, which is prime time for Jerusalem artichokes, you probably won't be able to find good fresh peas, but frozen petite peas do fine here. The vegetables are braised in butter and chicken stock until they produce a delicious glaze. I like the idea of fresh dill at the end, but minced parsley, scallions, or mint would be tasty, too. Serve with roast pork or ham or as a partner to lamb chops.

Serves 4

> 1 lemon
> 1 pound Jerusalem artichokes
> 1½ tablespoons butter
> Salt and freshly ground black pepper
> ½ cup chicken stock
> 5 ounces frozen petite peas *or* ¾ cup fresh peas
> 1 tablespoon minced fresh dill

1. Squeeze half the lemon and add the juice to a bowl of cold water. Peel the artichokes with a vegetable peeler and immediately drop them into the bowl to keep them from browning. When all the artichokes are peeled, remove them one by one from the water and cut them into ¾-inch chunks. Pat them dry.

2. Melt the butter in a large skillet over moderate heat. Add the artichokes and toss to coat them with butter. Season them with salt and pepper. Add a squeeze of lemon juice and the chicken stock. If using fresh peas, add them now. Bring the mixture to a simmer, cover, and reduce the heat. Simmer until the artichokes are crisp-tender, about 10 to 12 minutes. If using frozen peas, cook the artichokes until they are almost tender, then add the peas. The frozen peas are done as soon as they thaw.

3. When the artichokes and peas are done, uncover the skillet, raise the heat, and allow any remaining liquid to evaporate. When the cooking juices are reduced to a nice glaze, remove the skillet from the heat and stir in the dill. Taste and reseason if necessary; transfer to a warm serving bowl.

OTHER SERVING SUGGESTIONS

PAN ROASTED JERUSALEM ARTICHOKES Put scrubbed Jerusalem artichokes in the roasting pan alongside a chicken or pork loin, to cook in the roasting juices.

JERUSALEM ARTICHOKES IN CREAM Saute grated Jerusalem artichokes in enough butter to coat, then add cream and reduce until thick. Season with nutmeg.

BUTTERED JERUSALEM ARTICHOKES WITH HERBS Saute sliced Jerusalem artichokes in butter with minced dill, chives, parsley, or mint.

SWEET POTATOES

Is it a yam or a sweet potato? Even if it's labeled as a yam at the market, chances are it's a sweet potato. The true yam (genus *Dioscorea*) isn't widely seen in the U.S. except in Hispanic markets. Even the copper-skinned, orange-fleshed "garnet yam" is really a sweet potato.

Goodness knows why so many American cooks take something as naturally sweet as sweet potatoes and add marshmallows, honey, brown sugar, or maple syrup to them. In my kitchen, I like to cut the sweetness by pureeing them with another, less sweet vegetable, such as rutabaga (see page 137). If cooks would put aside the sugar and taste the vegetable *au naturel,* they would save themselves effort and calories and discover the true earthy, buttery, nutty sweet potato flavor.

TO SELECT   Sweet potatoes should be firm, with no soft or shriveled spots. Small to medium-size potatoes are usually the best quality.

TO STORE   Stored in a cool, humid place (not in the refrigerator), they should keep for at least a couple of weeks.

COOKING TIPS   ***Baking***   My favorite preparation is the simplest: bake sweet potatoes whole, unpeeled, in a preheated 400° oven until tender, then slit them open and fill them with butter. You can also bake chunks of peeled sweet potato alongside a roast. Before putting them in the pan, brush the chunks with melted butter to prevent discoloration; while they're cooking, turn them in the drippings occasionally.

Steaming   Steam peeled sweet potato chunks until tender, then toss them with butter. Boiled or steamed sweet potatoes can also be mashed or pureed with butter.

RUTABAGA-SWEET POTATO PUREE

These two root vegetables marry beautifully; the rutabaga moderates the candylike sweetness of the sweet potato and contributes needed body. Try it with pork loin or chops, a ham, or roast game. Note that you need a food mill for this dish as rutabagas can be fibrous.

Serves 6

1½ pounds rutabagas
1 pound sweet potatoes, peeled
4 to 5 tablespoons unsalted butter, in 4 or 5 slices
Pinch of allspice
Salt

1. Peel the rutabagas with a small, sharp knife. Usually the flesh just under the skin is tough, so peel thickly. You should have about one pound after peeling. Cut the rutabagas into large chunks and boil them in salted water until tender. Cooking time will depend on the size of your chunks, but 1-inch pieces will take about 30 minutes. Drain and put them through a food mill directly into a large saucepan.

2. Cut the sweet potatoes into chunks and boil them in salted water until tender. Cooking time will depend on the size of your chunks, but 1-inch pieces will take about 10 to 15 minutes. Drain and put them through the food mill into the same saucepan. Add the butter and reheat the vegetables over moderate heat, stirring until the butter is melted and the puree is hot throughout. Season with a pinch of allspice and salt to taste.

137

SWEET POTATOES, PARSNIPS, AND PEAS

Here is an enticing combination of autumn colors, textures, and tastes. Try it with a ham, a roast duck, a Thanksgiving turkey, or your Christmas goose. The dish is prettiest when made with the red-skinned, orange-fleshed garnet yams.

Serves 6

> ¾ **pound garnet yams**
> ¾ **pound parsnips**
> 1½ **cups shelled fresh peas (or one 10-ounce package frozen petite peas)**
> 2 **tablespoons butter**
> 2 **tablespoons minced parsley**
> **Salt and freshly ground black pepper**

1. Peel the yams and cut them into ½-inch cubes. Peel the parsnips and cut them into pieces approximately the same size as the yams.

2. Bring a couple of inches of salted water to a boil in the bottom of a steamer. If using fresh peas, put the yams, parsnips, and peas in the top of the steamer; cover and steam until the root vegetables are done but still firm, about 12 to 15 minutes. If using frozen peas, steam the yams and parsnips until they are just 2 or 3 minutes away from being done before adding the peas.

3. Transfer the vegetables to a warm serving bowl. Add the butter in thin slices, the parsley, and salt and pepper to taste. Toss gently.

WINTER

BROCCOLI	*Broccoli Stems, Mushrooms, and Peas*
	Broccoli and Potato Puree with
	Sour Cream and Dill
	Chopped Broccoli with Garlic
	and Pecorino
CABBAGE	*Steamed Cabbage with Sour Cream*
	and Paprika
	Braised Cabbage in Tomato Sauce
	Lemon Cabbage
	Braised Sauerkraut
	Braised Red Cabbage with Pancetta
CARDOON	*Braised Cardoon, Tomato, and*
	White Beans
CELERY ROOT	*Puree of Celery Root, Potato, and Turnip*
FENNEL	*Braised Fennel in Tomato Sauce*
	Fennel and Chick Peas
	Braised Fennel with Parmesan
GREENS	*Southern-Style Greens with Slab Bacon*
	Wilted Greens with Grated Feta
PARSNIPS	*Parsnips and Carrots in Cider*
RUTABAGAS	*Root Vegetable Hash*
SPINACH	*Spinach with Browned Garlic*
	Extra-Crusty Spinach Souffle
	Old-Fashioned Creamed Spinach
TURNIPS	*Shredded Turnips and Carrots*
	Braised Turnips

FOR VEGETABLE LOVERS, winter brings abundance—purple-tinged turnips and ruta-bagas; crisp cabbages, both red and green; vitamin-packed broccoli and leafy greens in tempting variety; the shapely bulb fennel with its licorice-like taste; giant stalks of prickly cardoon; and such deliciously edible roots as parsnips and celery root.

Compared to the tender, juicy produce of spring and summer, winter produce has substance. The root vegetables are dense, sturdy, earthy. Even the greens—the broccoli and cabbages, the collards and kale and spinach—have more aggressive flavor and firmer texture than the delicate peas, asparagus, and zucchini of warmer months.

Braising is often the method I choose for these firm, full-flavored winter vegeta-bles. Cooking vegetables and seasonings slowly in moist heat in a covered pot helps to knit flavors together and generates delicious pan juices. You end up with richer, deeper flavors and soft textures rather than crisp—the kind of food that appeals in cold weather. Nature seems to have planned for this; most winter vegetables do better in a braising pot than on a charcoal grill. Root vegetables, in particular, benefit from such treatment; chunks of turnip, rutabaga, or parsnip braised alongside a pot roast absorb the flavors of the meat and add their own sweet character to the cook-ing juices.

If you put up tomato sauce in summer, you can put it to good use in winter. I use tomato sauce as the braising liquid for cabbage (see page 152), cardoons, and fennel, simmering slowly until the vegetables are tender, then showering the dish with Parmesan. Often I add dried beans—white beans with cardoon (see page 158), chick peas with fennel (see page 167)—to make a hearty stew that eliminates the need to prepare a separate starch.

In winter, as always, I like to combine vegetables that seem to complement each other: broccoli stems with mushrooms; parsnips and carrots; turnips and car-rots; rutabagas, potatoes, and carrots. Try these combinations as presented in the following recipes and you'll no doubt find others that appeal to you, too.

BROCCOLI

More cooking sins are committed against broccoli than any other vegetable I can think of. It's so easy to cook right but just as easy to cook wrong, leaving you with waterlogged, strong-smelling, khaki-green stalks that nobody wants to eat.

Take pains to buy young, freshly harvested broccoli and pay attention to cooking times. Carefully purchased and carefully cooked, broccoli will be bright green, tender-crisp, and sweet. We all know it's on the list of "should-eat" vegetables, high in vitamins A and C, high in fiber, and low in calories. If you learn how to handle it, it will become a vegetable you *want* to eat—even with just a little coarse salt and a drizzle of good olive oil.

Some specialty markets carry broccoli Romanesco, a beautiful Italian variety. The cone-shaped head looks a bit like light green cauliflower, but look closer and you will see the pattern of fanciful spiral florets. It can be steamed or boiled and sauced or seasoned like broccoli or cauliflower. It has a more delicate, less cabbage-y taste and its unusual appearance makes it fun to serve.

TO SELECT   Look for broccoli with good color and compact, tightly closed florets. Yellowing buds or buds that look as if they are starting to flower mean the broccoli is too mature. Choose broccoli with thin stems when available; thick stems are often woody. Romanesco broccoli should be a compact head with tightly closed florets and an even green color.

TO STORE   Store broccoli in the refrigerator crisper in a perforated plastic bag and use within a day or two.

COOKING TIPS   ***Trimming***   Unless you are using very young broccoli, you will probably find that the stem has a thick skin and that the skin gets thicker and the stem gets woodier toward the base. If the base of the stem is thick and woody, cut it off. Peel the stem with a vegetable peeler or a small knife to reveal the pale green inner layer. If the stem is very thick, slit it in half from the end of the stalk to the base of the florets to allow steam to penetrate.

Some people prefer to cut off most of the stem and serve the florets with just a small bit of stem attached. If you do so, save the stems for Broccoli Stems, Mushrooms, and Peas (page 146). You can also separate the stems from the florets, peel the stems and chop them coarsely, then braise them along with the florets (see Chopped Broccoli with Garlic and Pecorino, (page 147).

Steaming vs. Boiling   There are at least two schools of thought about cooking broccoli. To maintain the vegetable's bright green color, the best approach is to boil it rapidly, uncovered, in a large quantity of salted water (the salt is for flavor; you may omit it). Cooking time will depend on the size of the stalks, but 3 to 5 minutes is about right. To test for doneness, slip a small knife into the thickest part of the stalk. It should be just barely tender. Boiling has two disadvantages compared to steaming. Timing is more critical—boiled florets quickly get waterlogged—and vitamin loss is greater.

Steamed vegetables retain more vitamins and better texture, but covering the pot, which you must do when steaming, promotes a chemical reaction that causes broccoli to turn khaki-green. Steaming also takes longer than boiling. Depending on size, broccoli stalks will take 6 to 10 minutes to become tender in a covered steamer set over, not in, boiling water.

I prefer to boil broccoli if I'm cooking large pieces and to steam it if I'm cooking small pieces. In your kitchen, the choice is yours.

BROCCOLI STEMS, MUSHROOMS, AND PEAS

A lot of people use broccoli florets and discard the tough stalks. But if the stalks are peeled, they're not tough at all—they're tender, sweet, and delicious. Serve the florets one day, steamed and tossed with olive oil, garlic, and Parmesan cheese; the next day, braise the stems with mushrooms and peas.

Serves 4 generously

> **8 ounces trimmed broccoli stalks (about 6 stalks)**
> **8 ounces large white cultivated mushrooms**
> **2 tablespoons unsalted butter**
> **Salt and freshly ground black pepper**
> **1 cup frozen petite peas or small fresh peas**
> **½ teaspoon fresh tarragon, minced**

1. Cut off the broccoli florets and save them for another use. With a vegetable peeler or a small sharp knife, pare the broccoli stalks down to the pale green, tender part. Be sure to remove all of the fibrous outer layer, leaving very tender stalks without any stringiness.

2. Wipe the mushrooms clean with a damp cloth. Trim away any brown, dried-out parts on the stem, then cut the mushrooms into quarters.

3. Heat 1½ tablespoons of butter in a large skillet over moderately high heat. Add the mushrooms and salt and pepper to taste. Cook until the mushrooms are nicely browned, about 20 minutes; shake the pan as necessary to keep the mushrooms from sticking and reduce the heat if necessary, but do not add any liquid. If using frozen peas, reduce the heat to moderate, add the peas, and cook, shaking the pan often, until they are thawed, about 2 minutes.

4. Bring a large pot of salted water to a boil. Add the broccoli stems and fresh peas (if using). Cook until the stems and peas are tender, about 5 minutes, then drain the vegetables well in a sieve and add them to the skillet. Add the tarragon and the remaining ½ tablespoon of butter. Cook over moderate heat until hot throughout; season to taste with salt and pepper.

VARIATION: In the spring try this dish with artichoke stems in place of the broccoli.

BROCCOLI AND POTATO PUREE WITH SOUR CREAM AND DILL

Potato gives this lovely puree body, but the broccoli flavor is paramount. Serve it with a steak, roast leg of lamb, or lamb or pork chops.

Serves 4

> **2½ tablespoons butter**
> **½ cup chopped onion**
> **1½ pounds broccoli**
> **One 6-ounce russet (baking) potato**
> **¼ cup sour cream**
> **1 tablespoon minced fresh dill**
> **Salt and freshly ground black pepper**

1. Melt 1½ tablespoons of butter in a skillet over medium-low heat. Add the onion and saute until softened, about 10 minutes. Set aside.

2. Remove the tough butt ends from the broccoli. Separate the florets from the stems. Remove the tough outer skin from the stems with a small sharp knife. Cut the stems into 1-inch lengths.

3. Fill a large pot with salted water. Peel the potato and put it in the water whole; bring the water to a boil over high heat. Partially cover the pot and lower the heat; simmer 12 minutes. Add the broccoli stems and cook until they are almost tender, about 6 to 8 minutes. Add the florets and cook until tender, about 5 minutes more. Drain the vegetables in a colander or sieve. Shake well to remove the excess water.

4. Put the broccoli, potato, onion, sour cream, and the remaining tablespoon of butter in a food processor and process until smooth. Add the dill and salt and pepper to taste; process until very smooth. Serve hot, in a warm bowl. If the puree has cooled down, you can reheat it in a double boiler over simmering water.

CHOPPED BROCCOLI WITH GARLIC AND PECORINO

Broccoli can stand up to assertive flavors, like the garlic, hot pepper flakes, and pecorino cheese used here. You can even add a little minced anchovy if you like. Try this with broiled veal chops with rosemary, a roast chicken infused with lemon, or pan-fried pork chops seasoned with juniper berries or fresh sage.

Serves 4

> 1 large bunch broccoli (about 1½ pounds)
> 2 tablespoons olive oil
> 2 cloves garlic, minced
> ⅛ to ¼ teaspoon hot red pepper flakes
> About 2 tablespoons chicken stock
> ½ cup grated pecorino cheese
> Salt

1. Separate the broccoli florets from the stalks. With a vegetable peeler or a small, sharp knife, remove the coarse outer layer of the stalks to reveal the pale green, tender heart. Cut the stalks into ½-inch lengths. Cut the florets into pieces approximately the same size as the stems, but keep them separate. You should have about 1 pound of broccoli after trimming.

2. Heat the olive oil in a large skillet over moderately low heat. Add the garlic and saute until fragrant, about 1 minute. Add the hot pepper flakes (use the full ¼ teaspoon if you want it really peppery), broccoli stems, and 1 tablespoon of chicken stock. Cover and cook until the broccoli stems are almost tender, about 5 to 7 minutes; add a bit more stock if necessary to keep the stems from sticking. Add the florets and the remaining tablespoon of stock; cover and cook until tender, about 5 minutes, shaking the skillet occasionally so that the broccoli cooks evenly. Transfer the broccoli to a warm serving bowl; sprinkle with cheese and salt to taste (be careful; the cheese is salty). Toss again, then serve.

OTHER SERVING SUGGESTIONS

BROCCOLI WITH HERBED LEMON BUTTER Dress cooked broccoli with melted butter flavored with lemon juice and minced dill or tarragon.

BROCCOLI WITH ANCHOVIES Broccoli and anchovies have a strong affinity. Try anchovy butter (see page 69) on steamed broccoli. Or make an anchovy sauce by mashing minced fillets to a paste in warm olive oil with minced garlic; add a squeeze of lemon juice at the end.

CHOPPED BROCCOLI WITH PARMESAN OR PINE NUTS Braise chopped broccoli and onions in butter, covering the skillet as necessary to cook the broccoli through, then sprinkle with grated Parmesan cheese or toasted pine nuts.

CABBAGE

Most well-stocked supermarkets carry at least four kinds of cabbage today: round red cabbage, Nappa cabbage (the elongated Chinese variety that's also sometimes spelled Napa), and two round green cabbages—the familiar smooth-leafed one and the crinkly-leafed Savoy. I'm not a big fan of Nappa cabbage (I find it watery and less flavorful than the others) so I haven't included any recipes for it; a good Chinese cookbook will tell you how to slice and stir-fry it. The other cabbages, however, are among the vegetables I like best. They are low in cost and calories, sweet and mild when young, and so amenable to different flavors and preparations that you can happily have cabbage for dinner twice a week.

TO SELECT   Cabbages should be firm and heavy for their size. The butt end should be moist, not dried out.

TO STORE   Refrigerate cabbages in your vegetable crisper. They will keep for at least a couple of weeks. It is advisable to keep them in a plastic bag because they emit odors that can spread to vegetables stored with them.

COOKING TIPS   **Cutting**   Remove any dirty or blemished outer leaves. Wash and dry the cabbage. Cut it in half through the core, then cut it into wedges of the desired size. To shred a cabbage, first cut it into quarters and remove the core; shred with a knife.

Steaming   I prefer to steam cabbage in a small amount of liquid; boiling makes it waterlogged and unpleasant. The recipe for Steamed Cabbage with Sour Cream and Paprika (page 150) can be used as a model for steaming wedges.

Braising   You can braise shredded cabbage in butter or olive oil in a covered skillet with no added liquid (see page 153), or you can braise it in tomato sauce (see page 152). When braising red cabbage, it's a good idea to add a little red wine or wine vinegar at the start to help preserve the red color; otherwise the cabbage turns a washed-out purple.

STEAMED CABBAGE WITH SOUR CREAM AND PAPRIKA

I love thick wedges of cabbage steamed just until they start to lose their crispness. The leftover steaming juices mixed with sour cream make an easy and delectable sauce. Pork chops, meat loaf, or smothered pork or veal cutlets would complement the cabbage.

Serves 4 to 6

> 1 small head green cabbage, about 1½ to 1¾ pounds
> ½ cup sour cream
> ½ cup chicken stock, plus more if needed
> 1½ tablespoons unsalted butter
> Salt (optional)
> Paprika

1. Cut the cabbage in half, then cut each half into 3 wedges of approximately equal size. Remove any raggedy outer leaves. Whisk the sour cream in a small bowl until smooth.

2. Lay the cabbage wedges in a heavy skillet in a single, tight-fitting layer. Add the chicken stock and bring to a simmer over moderately high heat. Cover, reduce the heat, and simmer until the cabbage is just tender, about 10 minutes.

3. While the cabbage steams, cut the butter into small pieces. Use tongs to transfer the cabbage wedges to a warm serving platter, allowing the excess liquid to drip back into the skillet. Immediately dot the cabbage with the butter. Add the liquid remaining in the skillet to the sour cream a little at a time, whisking until the mixture becomes pourable. If you do not have enough chicken stock left in the skillet to achieve the proper consistency, supplement it with additional chicken stock. Taste the sauce and add salt if needed; spoon it over the cabbage wedges. Sprinkle liberally with paprika and serve immediately.

VARIATION: If you prefer, you can omit the sour cream and dress the wedges with softened butter and minced dill, or spoon a little tomato sauce over them.

BRAISED CABBAGE IN TOMATO SAUCE

This recipe pays a dividend—it gives you more sauce than you need. Freeze the extra sauce and use it later to make the recipe again—speedily. Or braise green beans or cauliflower in the leftover sauce; it is versatile and delicious.

Pork chops or a pork roast would flatter the cabbage, but also consider an unsauced meat loaf, braised tongue, or sausage.

Serves 4 generously

TOMATO SAUCE WITH FENNEL
2 tablespoons olive oil
1 medium onion, chopped
1 medium carrot, peeled and finely diced
2 cloves garlic, minced
1 teaspoon fennel seeds
Large pinch hot red pepper flakes
28-ounce can plum tomatoes, with juice
1 teaspoon brown sugar, or more to taste
1 cup chicken stock
Salt

✿

1 pound green cabbage
Parmesan cheese
1 tablespoon minced parsley

1. First make the tomato sauce, as follows: Heat the olive oil in a 10-inch skillet over moderately low heat. Add the onion and carrot and saute until the vegetables soften, about 15 minutes. Add the garlic and saute until fragrant, about 1 minute. Crush the fennel seeds in a mortar; they do not have to be finely ground. Add them and the hot pepper flakes to the skillet. Break up the tomatoes by gently squishing them through your fingers; be careful not to splatter juice everywhere. Add the tomatoes with their juice to the skillet. Add 1 teaspoon brown sugar. Bring the mixture to a simmer, then reduce the heat and simmer, stirring occasionally, until the sauce is quite thick, about 30 minutes.

2. Puree the sauce in a food processor. Return it to the skillet and add the chicken stock. Simmer 5 minutes or until thickened; taste and adjust the seasoning, adding more fennel, some salt, or more sugar if needed. You will have about 3 cups.

152

3. Quarter and core the cabbage. Cut it into shreds about ¼ inch wide. Combine the cabbage and 1 cup of sauce in a 10- or 12-inch skillet. (Freeze the remaining sauce for later use.) Toss the cabbage with tongs to mix it well with the sauce. Resist the temptation to add liquid; the cabbage will generate its own. Cover and cook over moderately low heat, stirring occasionally, until the cabbage is quite tender, about 30 minutes. (Actual cooking time depends on the age of the cabbage.) Transfer the cabbage to a warm bowl or platter; garnish with a thick shower of grated Parmesan and the parsley.

LEMON CABBAGE

Braising shredded cabbage in butter without any additional liquid seems to preserve its sweet cabbage flavor. Using high enough heat to brown the cabbage slightly adds an appealingly nutty, brown-butter taste. Toss in some lemon zest, scallion, and parsley and you have an aromatic dish that flatters roast chicken, duck, or turkey; pork or ham in almost any guise; or a veal stew.

Serves 4

> 1 ½ tablespoons unsalted butter
> 1 ½ pounds shredded green cabbage (see Note)
> Salt and freshly ground black pepper
> ⅓ cup finely minced scallions (green onions)
> ½ teaspoon grated lemon zest, or more to taste
> 2 tablespoons minced parsley

Melt the butter in a large skillet over moderately high heat. Add the cabbage and season it with salt and pepper. Toss to coat the cabbage with butter. Cover and cook over moderately high heat, uncovering to stir once or twice, until the cabbage is lightly wilted and beginning to brown lightly in places, about 10 minutes. Watch carefully so the cabbage doesn't burn. Do not add any liquid. When the cabbage is just tender, remove the pan from the heat and immediately stir in the green onion and ½ teaspoon of grated lemon zest. Toss well. Taste and add more salt, pepper, or lemon zest if necessary. Stir in the parsley just before serving, saving a little to sprinkle on top.

NOTE: I find it best to shred the cabbage by hand; a food processor shreds it too fine.

BRAISED SAUERKRAUT

If you've had only badly cooked sauerkraut—limp, greasy, gray, and sour—you must make this dish. It is what braised sauerkraut should be: aromatic and mellow. Be sure to start with high-quality fresh sauerkraut, the refrigerated kind sold in delicatessens and good supermarkets. And don't eat it the day you make it; it is definitely better the second day.

Sauerkraut goes well with pork in almost any shape or form—sausages, pork chops, braised spareribs, a ham steak. This dish also would complement venison, goose, squab, pheasant, or wild boar.

Serves 4

> **1 pound fresh sauerkraut**
> **1 thick slice bacon, cut in half crosswise**
> **½ onion, thinly sliced**
> **2 cloves garlic, minced**
> **4 juniper berries**
> **1 bay leaf**
> **8 to 12 ounces smoked ham hock, in two pieces**
> **½ cup dry white wine**
> **1 cup chicken stock**

1. Preheat the oven to 325°. Rinse the sauerkraut under cold running water. Drain and squeeze it dry. Cook the bacon in a skillet over low heat until the slices are well rendered but not yet crisp. Transfer the slices to paper towels to drain.

2. Pour off all but 1½ tablespoons of bacon fat. Add the onion and saute until softened, about 5 minutes. Add the garlic and saute until fragrant, about 1 minute. Set aside.

3. Put the two rendered bacon pieces in the bottom of a lidded earthenware or ceramic baking dish with about a 6-cup capacity. Add the sauerkraut to the onion mixture in the skillet and toss it with tongs to blend. Transfer it to the baking dish; bury the juniper berries, bay leaf, and ham hocks in it. Pour the white wine and stock over the sauerkraut. Cover and bake 1½ hours. Cool in the dish, then refrigerate. The following day, reheat the sauerkraut in the covered dish in a 325° oven until hot throughout, about 30 minutes. If necessary, uncover the dish during the final 10 minutes to allow any excess liquid to evaporate.

BRAISED RED CABBAGE WITH PANCETTA

Most red cabbage recipes call for too much vinegar and too much sugar for my taste. I prefer a more wine-friendly preparation, with bay leaf and Italian unsmoked bacon (pancetta). A splash of balsamic vinegar at the end gives a subtle sweet-sour finish. Try it with pork, duck, calf's liver, or game.

Serves 4

> 2 teaspoons olive oil
> 2 ounces pancetta, finely minced
> ½ large yellow onion, finely minced
> 2 cloves garlic, minced
> 1½ pounds red cabbage, shredded
> 2 bay leaves
> 3 tablespoons balsamic vinegar (approximately)
> Freshly ground black pepper
> ¼ cup chicken stock
> Salt
> 2 tablespoons minced parsley

1. Heat the olive oil in a large heavy skillet over moderately low heat; swirl the skillet to coat it with oil. Add the pancetta and saute until it starts to crisp, about 3 to 4 minutes. Add the onion and saute until it softens, about 5 to 8 minutes. Add the garlic and saute until fragrant, about 1 minute. Add the cabbage, bay leaves, 1 tablespoon of balsamic vinegar, and several grindings of black pepper; toss with tongs to blend. Add the chicken stock and bring it to a simmer, then cover the pan and continue simmering, uncovering and stirring occasionally, until the cabbage is tender, about 15 to 20 minutes.

2. Uncover the pan and cook over moderately high heat until the excess liquid has evaporated. Remove the pan from the heat and season the cabbage to taste with salt and balsamic vinegar. Let it cool slightly, remove the bay leaves, taste it again, and reseason. Stir in 1½ tablespoons parsley. Transfer the cabbage to a warm serving platter or bowl and garnish with the remaining parsley.

OTHER SERVING SUGGESTIONS

QUICK BRAISED CABBAGE Braise shredded cabbage in butter with sliced onions and caraway seed. Or braise the shredded cabbage in butter with a little minced garlic and toss it with Parmesan cheese before serving.

See also Shredded Beets and Red Cabbage (page 46).

CARDOON

Unless you're an avid and curious cook, or have Italian relatives, you're probably not familiar with cardoon. It looks like overgrown celery and tastes something like artichoke—not surprising given that it's an artichoke relative. I had never seen or tasted cardoon until friends began inviting us to a yearly *bagna cauda,* an Italian feast featuring enormous platters of winter vegetables dipped in hot anchovy sauce. One of the guests grows a winter garden expressly for the party, and cardoon is always on his list. He serves just the tender inner ribs, to be dipped in the *bagna cauda,* a "hot bath" of olive oil, garlic, and mashed anchovy.

I don't have a great deal of experience in cooking cardoon, but I like it so much that I buy it whenever I find it. Even in northern California, that's not very often. If you live in an area with a significant Italian population, cardoon is likely to appear briefly in your markets in December and January. Some markets identify it by its Italian name, *cardoni.* Please seek it out, or grow your own, to discover how delicious it is when braised with Italian seasonings.

TO SELECT	Choose smallish cardoons over large, overgrown-looking ones. Avoid any that show signs of wilting or excessive browning, although the tips will be brown where the cardoon was cut.
TO STORE	Refrigerate in the vegetable crisper like celery, with the root end tucked into a plastic bag. It should last for about a week.
COOKING TIPS	See Braised Cardoon, Tomato, and White Beans (page 158) for a description of how to prepare cardoon.

BRAISED CARDOON, TOMATO, AND WHITE BEANS

Don't be put off by the length of this recipe; it is not a difficult dish and you are sure to succeed with it. It does take some time to prepare, but it can be done in stages and assembled in 5 minutes at dinner time. For that reason, and because it is so delicious and somewhat unusual, it's a great dish for dinner guests.

You will need some tomato sauce. You can use your own favorite recipe, but I particularly like the one described in Braised Cabbage in Tomato Sauce (page 152). Freeze the leftover sauce and use it to make the cabbage recipe or to braise cauliflower, green beans, or mushrooms. You also need to cook some white beans, which must first be soaked overnight. The beans can be cooked a day or two ahead; refrigerate them in their cooking liquid.

The cardoon is boiled with vinegar and flour to keep it from darkening. If you want to cook it a day ahead, drain it after cooking and refrigerate it in the ¾ cup of tomato sauce the recipe calls for.

Serve this lovely stew with a pork roast, roast chicken, or some fat, grilled sausages.

Serves 4

⅔ **cup dried Great Northern beans**
½**-pound piece smoked ham hock**
½ **onion stuck with 1 clove**
3 sprigs fresh thyme
1 bay leaf
1 lemon
1 small bunch cardoon
Salt
¼ **cup white wine vinegar**
¼ **cup all-purpose flour**
¾ **cup Tomato Sauce with Fennel (see page 152)**
Freshly ground black pepper
2 tablespoons minced parsley
Parmesan cheese

1. Cover the beans with cold water and soak overnight. Drain. Place the beans and 6 cups of cold water in a 4-quart saucepan. Add the ham hock, onion, thyme, and bay leaf. Bring to a simmer over moderately high heat, then reduce the heat to maintain a slow simmer. It is important to cook the beans slowly so they don't

burst open. Cook until the beans are just tender, about 1 hour. Let them cool in the liquid.

2. Fill a medium bowl with cold water and add the juice of the lemon. Discard the tough, stringy outer stalks of the cardoon to expose the pale inner stalks. Trim away any leafy parts. Use a vegetable peeler to peel the stalks, then cut them into ¾-inch lengths, beginning at the narrow end. When the stalk gets wide, halve it lengthwise, then continue cutting into ¾-inch lengths, so that you have pieces of approximately equal size. Drop the pieces into the acidulated water as you go.

3. Bring a large pot of salted water to a boil over high heat; add the wine vinegar. Put the flour in a small bowl; whisk in 1 cup of cold water, then add the mixture to the boiling water. The vinegar and flour will keep the cardoon from discoloring. When the water returns to a simmer, drain the cardoon pieces and add them to the pot. Reduce the heat and cook at a slow boil until the cardoon is tender. This can take anywhere from 30 minutes to 1¼ hours; test often. When the cardoon is done, drain thoroughly.

4. Transfer the cardoon to a 3-quart saucepan. Add the tomato sauce, 1½ cups of white beans (lift them out of the pot with a slotted spoon), and ¼ cup of the liquid from the beans. Season with salt and pepper. Reheat gently. Transfer to a warm serving bowl and garnish with minced parsley and a shower of Parmesan.

OTHER SERVING SUGGESTIONS

CARDOON WITH PARMESAN Boil cardoon until tender, then drain. Reheat in a saucepan with butter, salt, and pepper. Toss with grated Parmesan cheese before serving.

CARDOON IN CREAM Reheat boiled cardoon in cream with minced dill, parsley, chives, or nutmeg.

CELERY ROOT (CELERIAC)

The knobby celery root, with its rough brown skin and hairy root end, looks more formidable than it should. Underneath the thick skin, which peels easily with a knife, is smooth, cream-colored flesh as crisp as an apple and with an obvious celery taste. Cooking subdues the flavor a little, but not entirely. As generations of French cooks have proved, that subtle hint of celery is appealing in vegetable purees and winter stews.

TO SELECT

Large celery roots can be spongy at the heart. Choose smallish ones where possible, or buy a little extra so you can discard any spongy parts. Celery roots should feel firm and heavy for their size. For ease of peeling, look for relatively smooth ones. You lose about a third to a half of the root when you peel it; take that into account when figuring how much to buy.

TO STORE

Refrigerate in the vegetable crisper in a perforated plastic bag. It will keep for about a week.

COOKING TIPS

Trimming   Some markets have already trimmed away all trace of the celery stalks; if not, cut off any remaining parts of the stalks, then peel the roots to remove all traces of skin. Celery root quickly discolors after peeling. Put it in water acidulated with the juice of a lemon to prevent browning.

PUREE OF CELERY ROOT, POTATO, AND TURNIP

These three vegetables together make a delicious puree, with each one adding an important quality to the mix. The potato provides the body, the turnip a subtle sweetness, and the celery root its distinctive celery taste. French cooks make this sort of puree often and call it, generically, a "white puree." Pork, duck, and game are the usual partners.

Because celery root darkens quickly after peeling, peel it just before you're ready to put it in the boiling liquid. A little milk in the water helps keep the celery root white. Note that you need a food mill for this dish.

Serves 4

> ½ cup milk
> 1 large russet baking potato, about 10 ounces
> 12 ounces turnips
> 1 medium celery root, about 14 to 16 ounces
> 3 tablespoons butter
> ¼ cup cream (hot)
> Salt and freshly ground black pepper

1. Fill an 8-quart pot with salted water and add the milk. Bring to a simmer over moderately high heat.

2. Peel the potato and cut it in half lengthwise, then cut each half in half crosswise. Place the quarters in a bowl of cold water to prevent browning. Peel the turnips and cut them into pieces approximately the same size as the potato. Peel the celery root thickly with a knife, then cut it into 8 pieces. Add the celery root to the boiling liquid; when it returns to a boil, lower the heat and simmer 5 minutes. Add the potato and turnips and continue cooking until the vegetables are tender, about 15 minutes. Drain thoroughly, then return the vegetables to the pot and place it over low heat until any excess liquid has evaporated.

3. Set a food mill over a saucepan. Pass the vegetables through the mill into the saucepan. Place the pan over low heat. Add the butter and hot cream and stir briskly with a wooden spoon until the butter melts, the puree is smooth, and any excess liquid evaporates. Season highly with salt and pepper. Serve immediately.

OTHER SERVING SUGGESTIONS

CELERY ROOT REMOULADE You may have had this in restaurants. To make it, cut the peeled root into julienne strips with a mandoline (a French vegetable slicer) or by hand, or grate it coarsely in a food processor. Toss the raw celery root with a mustardy mayonnaise and minced parsley and let it marinate for several hours or a day before serving. It's a delicious side dish with roast chicken or baked ham.

CELERY ROOT-POTATO GRATIN Replace part of the potatoes in a potato gratin with sliced celery root.

BRAISED CELERY ROOT Braise cubed celery root in broth and butter until tender, then let the broth boil away to make a glaze.

FENNEL (FINOCCHIO, SWEET ANISE)

The popularity of Mediterranean, particularly Italian, cooking in this country has been a blessing for us fennel lovers. It's now a lot easier, at least where I live, to find fresh fennel in produce markets and I certainly see more restaurant chefs using it. With its pungent licorice flavor, fennel is not to everyone's taste. Cooking mutes that flavor, however, so try it cooked even if you're not fond of it raw.

TO SELECT

Fennel bulbs may have their stalks and some feathery leaves still attached in the market, or they may be trimmed down to the bulb. It doesn't matter from a quality standpoint, although it's nice to have the leaves for mincing and adding to other dishes. Smaller bulbs are more tender and less fibrous than larger ones. The outer layer of the bulb should be creamy white, not yellowing or browning, and with no deep cracks. If the outer layer is thick, old, and fibrous, you'll have to discard it, so try to find bulbs that look like they're young and tender.

TO STORE

Trim off the stalks, if any. Store the bulb in a perforated plastic bag in the refrigerator crisper, where it will keep for 3 or 4 days.

Braised Fennel with Parmesan

BRAISED FENNEL IN TOMATO SAUCE

Although fennel is most plentiful in winter, you do see it in some markets as early as September and as late as April. If you find fresh fennel and ripe tomatoes at the same time, take advantage of them with this recipe, which calls for fresh tomato sauce. While you're at it, make a double batch of the sauce and freeze it for future use. Using this recipe as a model, you could braise cabbage, cauliflower, celery, or eggplant in the sauce with good results. When fresh tomatoes aren't in season, you can use a sauce made from canned tomatoes according to your favorite recipe, or see page 152.

I would pair these tender, tomato-bathed wedges with pork chops, pan-fried sausages, or broiled chicken. Or omit the Parmesan and serve the fennel with meaty fish such as swordfish, tuna, or shark.

Serves 4

> 3 fennel bulbs (approximately 2 pounds total)
> 1 tablespoon olive oil
> Salt
> ½ cup chicken stock
> 1 cup Fresh Tomato Sauce (recipe follows)
> ½ cup grated Parmesan cheese

1. Cut off and discard the fennel stalks if they're still attached. Trim the base of each bulb and cut the bulbs into quarters through the base. Remove the outer layer if it looks tough or stringy (see illustration, page 168).

2. Heat the olive oil in a large heavy skillet over moderately high heat. Place the fennel in the skillet in one tight layer. Brown the wedges on one cut side, then turn them to brown the other cut side. Turn the wedges browned sides up and season them lightly with salt. Add the stock and tomato sauce. Cover and simmer over moderately low heat until the fennel is tender, about 20 minutes. Uncover, raise the heat to moderate, and simmer about 10 minutes to reduce the sauce.

3. Transfer the fennel to a warm serving platter. Raise the heat to high and simmer the sauce until it is quite thick, then spoon it over the fennel. Shower with grated Parmesan.

FRESH TOMATO SAUCE

I particularly like this sauce, adapted from a Marcella Hazan recipe, because you don't have to peel the tomatoes. It can be frozen successfully or canned according to conventional canning methods. If you have a large enough saucepan, make a double batch. Note that you need a food mill for this recipe.

Makes about 1½ cups

2 pounds ripe tomatoes
¼ cup olive oil
⅓ cup minced onion
⅓ cup minced celery
⅓ cup minced carrot
4 to 5 sprigs fresh thyme
1 bay leaf
1 large clove garlic, minced
Pinch of hot red pepper flakes (optional)
1 teaspoon brown sugar (optional)
Salt

1. Wash and dry the tomatoes. Quarter them (no need to core) and put them in a 4-quart saucepan. Cover and cook over moderate heat until they have softened slightly and rendered a lot of juice, about 10 minutes. Uncover and simmer, stirring occasionally, until the tomatoes are reduced to a thick sauce, about 1¼ hours. Puree the sauce in a food mill.

2. Heat the olive oil in a heavy 10-inch skillet over moderate heat. Add the onion, celery, carrot, thyme sprigs, and bay leaf. Cook, stirring occasionally, until the vegetables are softened, about 20 minutes. Add the garlic and cook until fragrant, about 1 minute. Add the tomato puree, and hot pepper flakes if you like a sauce with a touch of heat. Bring to a simmer. Taste and add brown sugar if you think the sauce needs a hint of sweetness. Simmer, stirring often to prevent sticking, until the sauce reaches the desired consistency, about 10 minutes. Season to taste with salt.

FENNEL AND CHICK PEAS

Even those who find the licorice flavor of fennel too dominating on its own will probably enjoy this juicy stew. Try it with roast pork, pan-fried sausage, or a meaty baked fish such as tuna, sea bass, or swordfish. For convenience and best flavor, cook the chick peas a day ahead. Then all you have to do is add the fennel and simmer briefly.

Serves 4 to 6

> ¾ cup dried chick peas (garbanzo beans)
> ½-pound piece smoked ham hock or slab bacon
> ½ onion stuck with 1 clove
> 3 sprigs fresh thyme
> 1 bay leaf
> 12 ounces fennel, after trimming (2 to 3 bulbs)
> 2 cloves garlic, minced
> Salt and freshly ground black pepper
> 1 tablespoon minced parsley
> 2 tablespoons minced fresh fennel leaves (optional)

1. Soak the chick peas covered with cold water overnight, then drain. Put the chick peas and 8 cups of cold water in a 4-quart saucepan; add the ham hock, onion, thyme, and bay leaf. Bring to a simmer; reduce the heat and continue simmering until the chick peas are just tender, about 1½ to 2 hours. Add more boiling water if necessary to keep the chick peas covered. When they are done, let them cool in the cooking liquid, then refrigerate. This can—and indeed should—be done a day ahead.

2. Cut away and discard the fennel stalks, reserving any feathery leaves. Cut the bulbs into quarters; trim away some of the core, leaving enough to hold the bulb intact. If the bulbs have a tough, thick outer layer, pull it back and discard it; use only the pale green tender part. Chop the fennel into ½-inch pieces.

3. Remove the ham hock, bay leaf, onion, and thyme sprigs from the chick peas. Bring the chick peas to a simmer over moderate heat. Add the fennel, garlic, and salt and pepper to taste; stir once, then partially cover and cook until the fennel is tender, about 10 to 15 minutes; check often. Taste and reseason. Transfer the stew to a warm serving bowl and garnish with parsley and, if available, minced fennel leaves.

BRAISED FENNEL WITH PARMESAN

These butter-browned fennel wedges braised in stock are compatible with almost any meat that has an Italian flavor. Try them with rosemary-seasoned veal chops or lamb chops, braised lamb shoulder, meat loaf, or a tomato-sauced chicken dish.

Serves 4

> 2 medium or 3 small bulbs fennel
> 1 tablespoon butter
> 1 tablespoon olive oil
> Salt and freshly ground black pepper
> 1 clove garlic, peeled and halved
> ½ cup chicken or veal stock
> ⅓ cup freshly grated Parmesan cheese
> 1 tablespoon minced parsley

1. Cut off and discard the fennel stalks if they're still attached. Trim the base of each bulb and cut the bulbs into quarters through the base. Remove the outer layer if it looks tough or stringy.

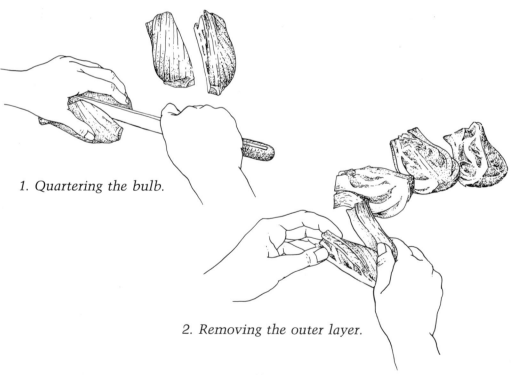

1. Quartering the bulb.

2. Removing the outer layer.

2. Heat the butter and oil over moderate heat in a heavy skillet just large enough to hold the fennel in one layer. When the fat begins to sizzle, add the fennel, one cut side down. Season with salt and pepper. Cook until lightly browned, about 10 minutes, then turn the other cut side down and brown lightly, about 5 minutes. Add the garlic and stock; cover and simmer until the bulbs are tender, about 20 to 25 minutes. Watch closely and don't overcook the fennel or it will be mushy.

3. When the bulbs are just tender, uncover the skillet and simmer until the liquid is reduced to a syrupy glaze. Transfer the fennel to a warm serving platter; discard the garlic. Sprinkle with Parmesan and garnish with parsley.

OTHER SERVING SUGGESTIONS

FENNEL AND RADISH SALAD If you are having a winter picnic with some cold roast pork or pork sandwiches, a fennel salad would be a fine side dish. Slice fennel paper-thin, then toss it with some sliced radishes, some minced chives or sliced red onion, and a mustard vinaigrette.

POTATO-FENNEL GRATIN Use thin slices of fennel to replace some of the potato slices in a potato gratin.

BRAISED FENNEL Fennel can be braised in stock, alone (see Braised Fennel with Parmesan, page 168) or in combination with other vegetables such as carrots or peas. Or you can braise it in tomato sauce or chicken stock then garnish with Parmesan cheese. Tuck fennel wedges around a pot roast or add them to your favorite stew.

GREENS FOR COOKING

Nutritionists are constantly urging us to eat more leafy greens, but they don't need to twist my arm. Cooked greens make regular appearances on my dinner table; they cook so quickly and demand so little in the way of preparation or seasoning that I turn to them often when I'm too busy or tired to make much of an effort. That they are generally rich in vitamins A and C, calcium, iron, and fiber is just one more reason to love these sweet, earthy-tasting vegetables.

You can successfully cook almost any leafy green, including tender butter lettuce, but the greens I'm referring to here are the sturdy, dark green greens that don't taste good raw (unless they're very young). Collard greens, turnip greens, mustard greens, beet greens, and kale are among the greens I include in the following comments. Chard could arguably be included as well, but its peak season is summer so you will find it discussed separately in the summer chapter (page 67). The cooked-greens recipes in this book specify which greens to use, but you can take liberties. Collard greens and kale are closely related and can substitute for each other; the same goes for beet greens and chard.

TO SELECT   It sounds obvious, but greens should be fresh looking. They shouldn't have any slimy or wilted parts, and they should have good, full color with no yellowing. In general, greens get stronger or hotter tasting and tougher as they get older and larger; for sweetest flavor, look for greens on the young side.

TO STORE   Because of their high moisture content, greens are not great keepers; they soon go limp. Store them in a perforated plastic bag in the refrigerator and use them within 3 to 4 days.

COOKING TIPS   **Washing**   To wash greens, fill the sink with cold water. Add the greens and swish them several times to dislodge any dirt. Lift the greens out of the water and drain them in a colander. If the water looks dirty, drain and refill the sink and repeat the process.

Trimming   Most of these greens have tough central stems or ribs that should be separated from the leaves before cooking. You can strip the leaves away by hand or with a knife.

Boiling   The most basic preparation is to boil the greens until tender in a large quantity of salted water, then drain them.

Seasoning   Compatible seasonings for greens include sauteed onion and garlic and chopped fresh herbs such as mint, dill, or cilantro. Let your menu guide you in choosing seasonings. If you're serving an Italian fennel sausage, you might season the greens with garlic and Parmesan; if you're serving them with baked ham, you might season them "Southern style," with bacon fat and hot pepper vinegar.

SOUTHERN-STYLE GREENS WITH SLAB BACON

These irresistible greens are absolutely better the second day. They seem to absorb more of the smoky bacon flavor, and the braising liquid ("pot likker") tastes better, too. In contrast to what you're served in some restaurants, greens prepared this way are neither salty nor greasy. You can almost taste the nutrition in them. Don't throw away the pot liquor. Use it in vegetable soup or enjoy a cup of it for lunch the next day.

Serves 4

> **½ pound slab bacon (not salt pork), in one piece**
> **2 pounds collard greens or turnip greens**
> **2 cloves garlic, peeled and sliced thin**
> **Salt and freshly ground black pepper (optional)**
> **Hot pepper vinegar**

1. Put the bacon in a large pot. Add 3 quarts of cold water and bring it to a simmer over moderately high heat. Reduce the heat and continue simmering until the liquid is reduced to about 5 cups. This will take about 1½ hours, depending on the size and shape of your pot.

2. Meanwhile, wash the greens well and let them drain (no need to dry them). Remove and discard the stems. Stack the leaves and slice them crosswise at 1-inch intervals. When the stock is ready, add the garlic then add the greens a few at a time, poking them down into the liquid with a wooden spoon until they wilt. When all the greens have been added, cook them at a simmer until tender, about 30 to 40 minutes. Stir occasionally to keep the greens below the surface of the liquid. Let them cool in the liquid.

3. To serve, reheat the greens in their liquid; season if necessary with salt and black pepper. Serve in warm bowls, with a smidgen of the bacon and some of the braising liquid (pot liquor). Offer hot pepper vinegar on the side.

Braised Turnips (page 189),
bottom: Southern-Style Greens with Slab Bacon

WILTED GREENS WITH GRATED FETA

The sharp, salty taste of feta cheese gives cooked greens just the kick they need. Serve these with pork loin roasted with bay leaves, pan-fried sausage, or chicken baked or roasted with lemon and oregano.

Serves 4

> **12 ounces kale**
> **12 ounces collard greens**
> **1½ tablespoons olive oil**
> **½ cup minced scallions (green onions)**
> **2 cloves garlic, finely minced**
> **Salt and freshly ground black pepper**
> **1½ tablespoons minced fresh dill**
> **4 ounces Greek feta cheese, preferably in one firm piece**

1. Remove and discard the coarse ribs from both the kale and the collard greens. Wash the greens well in cold water; drain.

2. Bring a large pot of salted water to a boil over high heat. Add the greens and stir to wilt them. Cook until they are limp and tender, about 10 minutes, then drain them in a colander and run cold water over them to stop the cooking process. Drain again, pressing on the greens with a rubber spatula to release any excess moisture. When they are cool, chop them coarsely.

3. Heat the olive oil in a large skillet over moderate heat. Add the scallions and saute until they soften, about 3 to 5 minutes. Add the garlic and saute until fragrant, about 1 minute. Stir in the greens. Season to taste with salt and pepper and cook, stirring, until hot throughout. Stir in the dill and transfer the greens to a warm serving bowl or platter. Using the medium-fine side of a grater, shred half the feta evenly over the greens and toss it in gently; shred the remaining feta on top. Serve immediately.

OTHER SERVING SUGGESTIONS

SIMPLE DRESSED GREENS Chop boiled and drained greens and reheat them in butter, olive oil, or bacon fat. A little lemon juice, wine vinegar, or hot pepper vinegar is usually desirable at the end.

PARSNIPS

Parsnips resemble pale yellow carrots. They have a sweet, nutty flavor and starchy texture that reminds me of sweet potato with a hint of celery root. For something that tastes so good, they are surprisingly little used. I know my mother never prepared them, and I don't recall what it was that compelled me, as an adult, to buy some and cook them—curiosity, I suppose, and an open mind about vegetables. If you haven't tried parsnips, buy a few the next time you see them. Steam them, toss them with butter, salt, and pepper and see if you haven't discovered something new and delicious.

TO SELECT

Parsnips should feel firm, not spongy or flabby. Avoid overly large ones; they tend to have woody cores. To minimize waste, I look for parsnips that have the most even, carrot-like shape and tend to avoid those that have very large tops that narrow down to skinny tips.

TO STORE

Refrigerate parsnips in a perforated plastic bag. They will keep for at least a couple of weeks.

COOKING TIPS

Trimming Peel parsnips with a vegetable peeler and trim the ends. Cut them into pieces of approximately equal size. Like carrots, parsnips have a central core. If the core looks woody, as it sometimes does if the parsnips are large, cut it out.

PARSNIPS AND CARROTS IN CIDER

I've never been a fan of recipes that call for lots of sugar with carrots and beets. I'd rather bring out their natural sweetness through roasting or braising. Here, a dash of apple cider makes a braising liquid for carrots and parsnips, with apple brandy added at the end to create an aromatic glaze. The orange carrots and pale yellow parsnips look beautiful together and are compatible with pork, ham, duck, rabbit, or turkey.

Serves 4

> ¾ **pound parsnips**
> ¾ **pound carrots**
> 1½ **tablespoons butter**
> **Salt and freshly ground black pepper**
> ½ **cup sparkling apple cider**
> 3 **tablespoons Calvados or apple brandy**
> 1 **tablespoon minced parsley (optional)**

1. Preheat the oven to 425°. Peel the parsnips and carrots and trim the ends. Cut them into batons about 1½ to 2 inches long and ½ inch thick. The exact size isn't important as long as they are of equal size so they will cook evenly.

2. Use 2 teaspoons of the butter to grease a heavy baking dish that is just large enough to hold the vegetables in one layer. Arrange the vegetables in the dish, season with salt and pepper to taste, and dot with the remaining butter. Pour in the cider, cover the baking dish tightly with a lid or aluminum foil, and bake 15 minutes. Uncover and use a metal spatula to turn the vegetables over in the juices. Recover and continue baking 15 minutes. Uncover and bake an additional 10 minutes to allow the juices to reduce and glaze the vegetables. At the end of the cooking time, the vegetables should be tender and the cooking juices reduced to a glaze.

3. Remove the dish from the oven and immediately sprinkle the Calvados over the vegetables. Shake the dish gently to coat the vegetables with the Calvados-flavored juices. Transfer the vegetables to a warm serving bowl, scraping all the juices from the pan with a rubber spatula. Garnish with parsley if desired.

OTHER SERVING SUGGESTIONS

BRAISED PARSNIPS Cut the trimmed parsnips into pieces of the desired size. Heat some butter in a skillet over moderately low heat. Add the parsnips, toss to coat them with butter, and season them with salt and pepper. Cover and cook over low heat until tender. Sprinkle with chopped parsley before serving.

MASHED PARSNIPS Boil the parsnips in a large quantity of salted water until tender. Drain thoroughly and mash or puree with butter, milk or cream, salt, and pepper.

STEAMED PARSNIPS Steam the parsnips over simmering water in a vegetable steamer. When tender, dress them with butter, salt, pepper, and a pinch of mace or nutmeg.

ROASTED PARSNIPS Parsnips in large chunks can be arranged around a covered pot roast or an uncovered roast. In the latter case, baste them occasionally with the cooking juices to keep them moist.

PARSNIP PUREE Parsnips make delicious purees, on their own or in combination with other root vegetables such as carrots, potatoes, rutabagas, sweet potatoes, or winter squash (see Autumn Squash and Parsnip Puree, page 129).

RUTABAGAS

Here's another for the list of underappreciated vegetables, one that I'm sure people would like if they would just give it an open-minded try. I suspect that a lot of people who turn up their noses at rutabagas haven't tasted them.

Thought to be a cross between a turnip and a wild cabbage, the rutabaga has dense yellow flesh—more dense than a turnip—and a sweet, buttery, nutty flavor. At least a young rutabaga tastes that way. An old, overgrown rutabaga will lose its sweetness and become almost peppery-hot.

TO SELECT   Choose small rutabagas over large ones. Large ones tend to be less sweet and can have spongy interiors. Rutabagas should feel heavy for their size and firm.

TO STORE   Ideally, rutabagas should be stored in a cool, dark, humid place, such as a root cellar. Lacking that, refrigerate them; they will keep for about three weeks.

COOKING TIPS   **Trimming**   Rutabagas need to be thickly peeled with a small, sharp knife. If you don't get all the skin off, you will be left with some unpleasantly tough parts when the rutabagas are cooked. After peeling, cut them into the desired shape: slices, cubes, or julienne strips.

Braising   Braise rutabagas in butter in a covered skillet with a little bit of water or stock.

Boiling   Boil rutabagas in a large quantity of salted water, then drain. Boiled rutabagas can be mashed with butter or tossed in butter, alone or with other vegetables (see Root Vegetable Hash, page 180).

Steaming   Rutabagas can be steamed over simmering water in a covered steamer, although this takes a long time because they are dense.

Roasting   Arrange rutabaga wedges around a pot roast or an uncovered roast. In the latter case, they should be basted occasionally to keep them from drying out.

ROOT VEGETABLE HASH

This straightforward, old-fashioned recipe is one of my vegetable favorites. If you appreciate simple dishes, you'll know you just can't make anything better to serve with a pot roast or a stew.

Serves 4

> **1 pound rutabagas**
> **⅔ pound carrots**
> **⅔ pound red-skinned potatoes**
> **3 tablespoons butter**
> **Salt and freshly ground black pepper**
> **1 tablespoon minced parsley (optional)**

1. Peel the rutabagas, removing all traces of the thick skin. Cut them into ½-inch cubes. Peel the carrots and slice them about ½ inch thick. Scrub the potatoes well but do not peel them; cut them into pieces about the same size as the rutabagas.

2. Bring a large pot of salted water to a boil over high heat. Add the rutabagas and cook 5 minutes, then add the remaining vegetables and cook until they are soft enough to mash but not mushy, about 15 more minutes. Drain thoroughly in a colander.

3. Put the hot vegetables in a clean pot and shake the pot over moderate heat until the vegetables are completely dry. Remove the pot from the heat, add the butter in small pieces, and mash the vegetables gently with a potato masher; they should be mashed, not pureed. Season to taste with salt and pepper. Transfer to a warm serving bowl. Garnish with parsley if desired.

OTHER SERVING SUGGESTIONS

See Rutabaga-Sweet Potato Puree (page 137)

SPINACH

When in doubt, serve spinach. It's an appealing companion to every type of meat, poultry, or fish I can think of, from sole to wild boar. With rich main courses, prepare it simply—wilted with olive oil or butter and seasoned perhaps with charred garlic (page 183). With chops, roasts, or other unsauced meats, try old-fashioned creamed spinach (page 186) or a crusty spinach souffle (page 185).

TO SELECT
Choose young spinach with small leaves and thin stems over older spinach with horsey leaves and thick stems. Older spinach leaves are tougher and have a stronger flavor. Avoid any bunches that contain wilted, yellowing, or slimy leaves.

TO STORE
Refrigerate spinach in the vegetable crisper in a plastic bag and use it within 2 to 3 days.

COOKING TIPS
Trimming Remove coarse spinach stems by slicing straight across the bunch at the point where the leaves meet the stem; you won't get all the stem on all the leaves, but you will get most of it. If you have bought loose spinach (not tied in a bunch), you may find it easier to remove the stems by hand. Hold the leaf in one hand and bend it in half along its length; with the other hand, pull the stem toward you.

Spinach needs careful washing to remove any grit. Fill a sink with cold water. Put the leaves in the sink and swish them several times to dislodge dirt. After washing, remove by hand any large stems that you didn't get the first time. Lift the spinach out into a colander. If the water is dirty, drain the sink and repeat the washing.

Steaming You can cook spinach leaves in a large covered pot, in just the water clinging to the leaves. Set the pot over moderate heat and cook 3 to 5 minutes, depending on how much spinach is in the pot. Uncover it once or twice and toss the leaves with tongs so that they wilt evenly. Drain.

Blanching I prefer a method which cooks spinach more quickly and evenly than steaming and preserves its color, flavor, and texture better. Bring a large pot of salted water to a boil over high heat. Add the spinach leaves and stir them down with a wooden spoon until they collapse and are covered by water; this will take just a few seconds. Immediately drain the leaves in a sieve. Flush them with cold running water to stop the cooking, then drain again. Squeeze the spinach dry and it is ready to be reheated in olive oil or butter with the seasonings of your choice. After spinach has been wilted, drained, and squeezed dry, you can refrigerate it for up to two days in an airtight container.

SPINACH WITH BROWNED GARLIC

This simple dish depends on the nutty, caramelized flavor of lightly browned garlic. Make sure the garlic is fresh and sweet, not old, hot, and sprouting. With the Parmesan cheese, this dish would complement almost any meat, including veal chops or sauteed veal scallops, pork roast or pork scallops, baked chicken, or meat loaf. Without the cheese, it could accompany baked, broiled, or grilled fish, preferably full-flavored varieties like swordfish, shark, and tuna.

Serves 4

> **2½ pounds fresh spinach**
> **8 cloves garlic**
> **2½ tablespoons olive oil**
> **Salt and freshly ground black pepper**
> **Grated Parmesan cheese (optional)**

1. Trim and wash the spinach (see page 181). Bring a large pot of salted water to a boil over high heat. Add the spinach leaves and stir to wilt them. Cook until they are just barely limp, about 30 seconds, then drain them in a colander and run cold water over them to stop the cooking process. Drain again. Squeeze the spinach gently between your hands to remove the excess liquid.

2. Peel the garlic cloves and slice them lengthwise about ⅛ inch thick. Heat the olive oil in a large skillet over moderate heat. Add the garlic and cook, stirring or shaking the skillet often, until the slices start to brown lightly; adjust the heat as necessary to prevent them from burning. It should take about 3 to 5 minutes for the garlic to soften and become golden brown.

3. Add the spinach. Toss the spinach with tongs to coat the leaves with oil and to separate them. Season to taste with salt and pepper, and cook until hot throughout. Transfer to a warm serving bowl; if desired, top with grated Parmesan cheese.

EXTRA-CRUSTY SPINACH SOUFFLE

You don't need a high-sided souffle dish to make a great souffle. Baked on an oven-proof platter or in a low-sided gratin dish, a souffle will still rise dramatically, but it will have proportionately more crusty outside to creamy interior. That's the way I like it.

Try this fluffy spinach souffle with leg of lamb, pan-fried chicken breasts, or a veal roast. You have to use a lot of pots to make this dish, but I think it's worth it.

Serves 4 to 6

> **12 ounces fresh spinach (approximately)**
> **4 tablespoons plus 1 teaspoon unsalted butter**
> **¼ cup plus 5 tablespoons grated Parmesan cheese**
> **3 tablespoons flour**
> **1 cup milk**
> **¼ teaspoon nutmeg, preferably freshly grated**
> **4 large eggs, separated, plus 1 extra white**
> **¾ teaspoon salt**
> **Freshly ground black pepper**

1. Trim and wash the spinach (see page 181). Bring a large pot of salted water to a boil. Add the spinach and stir until the leaves collapse and are totally immersed in water. Drain them in a sieve; flush with cold running water to stop the cooking process. Drain again.

2. Use 1 teaspoon of butter to grease the bottom and sides of an ovenproof platter or a 13-inch oval gratin dish. Coat the platter or dish with 3 tablespoons of Parmesan cheese. Set aside.

3. Preheat the oven to 425°. Melt the remaining 4 tablespoons of butter in a medium saucepan over moderately low heat. Add the flour and whisk to blend; cook, whisking constantly, for about 1 minute. Whisk in the milk. Bring the mixture to a simmer, whisking, then reduce the heat to low. Stir in the nutmeg. Cook, whisking occasionally, for about 5 minutes to allow the mixture to thicken and lose its raw flour taste. Remove it from the heat and let it cool 10 minutes, then whisk in the 4 egg yolks one at a time. Whisk in ¼ cup of Parmesan, the salt, and several grinds of pepper. Transfer the mixture to a large bowl.

4. Squeeze the spinach between your hands to remove as much excess liquid as possible. Measure out ⅓ cup of tightly packed leaves and put them in a food processor with half of the sauce; puree thoroughly, stopping the machine once or twice to scrape down the sides. Do not be tempted to use the excess spinach; it will make the souffle heavy. Stir the spinach puree into the remaining sauce.

5. Beat the 5 egg whites to firm but not stiff peaks. Fold half of the whites into the spinach mixture to lighten it, then gently fold in the rest. Transfer the mixture to the prepared platter or baking dish. Top with the remaining Parmesan. Bake 18 minutes, at which point the souffle should be puffy and lightly browned on top. Serve immediately.

OLD-FASHIONED CREAMED SPINACH

It's an old-fashioned idea but a new recipe, designed to minimize the use of flour and maximize the fresh spinach taste. The result is a silky smooth, creamy dish without the pasty quality that too many older versions have. Enjoy it with leg of lamb, prime rib, roast chicken, or a crown roast of pork.

Serves 4

> **2 pounds fresh spinach**
> **1½ tablespoons butter**
> **1½ tablespoons flour**
> **¾ cup milk**
> **¼ cup heavy cream**
> **Salt and freshly ground black pepper**
> **Freshly grated nutmeg**

1. Trim and wash the spinach (see page 181). Bring a large pot of salted water to a boil over high heat. Add the spinach leaves and stir to wilt them. Cook until they are just barely limp, about 30 seconds, then drain them in a colander and run cold water over them to stop the cooking process. Drain again. Squeeze the spinach gently between your hands to remove the excess liquid. (Spinach doesn't have to be completely dry, but it shouldn't be wet.) Chop it fine.

2. In a medium saucepan, melt the butter over moderately low heat. Add the flour and whisk to blend; cook 1 minute. Add the milk, whisking constantly, then add

the cream. Bring to a simmer, whisking, then reduce the heat to low and cook, whisking often, until the mixture is thick and smooth and no longer tastes floury, about 5 minutes. Season highly with salt, pepper, and freshly grated nutmeg.

3. Add the chopped spinach to the cream sauce and stir with a wooden spoon to blend. Cook over low heat until the flavors marry, about 8 to 10 minutes; taste and reseason as necessary. Transfer to a warm serving bowl.

OTHER SERVING SUGGESTIONS

BUTTERED SPINACH Reheat blanched and chopped spinach in butter. Season it with grated Parmesan cheese, or add cream and simmer until it thickens.

TURNIPS

They're almost always inexpensive, but turnips aren't just for humble meals. Braised in butter and meat stock to a glazed golden brown (see page 189), they can flatter a crown roast of pork, a leg of lamb, or a stately prime rib. Young turnips have a sweet and subtly peppery taste that is especially appealing with "sweet" meats like pork and duck. Try them boiled and mashed with potatoes and butter, or shredded with carrots and sauteed in butter (see page 188) until they hover between crisp and tender.

TO SELECT   Choose small turnips over large ones. Large ones can be spongy inside and tend to be hot. Turnips should feel heavy for their size and firm, not spongy.

TO STORE   Ideally, turnips should be stored in a cool, dark, humid place, such as a root cellar. Lacking that, refrigerate them in the vegetable crisper; they will keep for about a week.

COOKING TIPS   ***Peeling and Cutting***   Peel young turnips with a vegetable peeler. Older turnips have thicker skins that need to be peeled with a knife. Before cooking, slice them, cut them into chunks or small dice, or grate them.

Cooking   Braise turnips in a covered skillet with butter and a little stock. They can also be boiled or steamed.

SHREDDED TURNIPS AND CARROTS

This dish takes all of five minutes to prepare and about 15 minutes to cook. You'll love the contrast of sweet carrots with peppery turnips, two flavors that together flatter pork in any form—roast loin, braised shoulder, pan-fried chops, or a baked ham.

Serves 4

½ **pound carrots**
¾ **pound turnips**
2 **tablespoons unsalted butter**
Salt and freshly ground black pepper
1 **tablespoon minced fresh dill, mint, or parsley**

1. Peel the carrots and remove the tops and tips. Peel the turnips thickly; you should have about 8 ounces of turnips after peeling. Using the coarse grating blade of a food processor or a box grater, grate the carrots and turnips together.

2. Melt the butter in a large skillet over moderate heat. Add the carrots and turnips, season generously with salt and pepper, toss to coat them with butter, then cover. Cook, stirring occasionally, until the vegetables are just tender, about 15 minutes. Uncover, stir in the herbs and taste for seasoning. Serve immediately.

BRAISED TURNIPS

Sometimes the simplest ways are the best, as with these browned and braised turnips that glaze in their own sweet juices. Why fuss with a good thing? A pork or lamb stew or roast duck would be an appealing partner.

Serves 4

>1¼ pounds turnips (approximately)
>1 tablespoon butter
>1 tablespoon olive oil
>Salt and freshly ground black pepper
>½ cup chicken stock
>1 tablespoon minced fresh mint, dill, chives, parsley, or a combination

1. Peel the turnips thickly with a paring knife; you should have about 1 pound after peeling. Cut the turnips into wedges of approximately equal size, by quartering medium-size turnips from top to root or cutting larger turnips into sixths.

2. Heat the butter and olive oil in a heavy 10-inch skillet over moderate heat. Add the turnips, one cut side down, and saute until lightly browned on that side, about 8 to 10 minutes. Season with salt and pepper. With tongs, turn the turnips to place the other cut side down and cook 5 minutes. Add the stock, cover, and simmer until the turnips are just tender. The time will depend on the size of the wedges, but 2-inch turnips, quartered, will take about 15 minutes. Slip a paring knife in and out to test for doneness. When just done, uncover the skillet, raise the heat, and simmer until the stock is reduced to a syrupy glaze. Transfer the turnips to a warm serving platter and sprinkle with herbs.

OTHER SERVING SUGGESTIONS

ROAST TURNIPS Arrange turnip wedges around a pot roast or an uncovered roast; in the latter case, baste occasionally to keep them from drying out.

PARTNERS Turnips combine well with other root vegetables (potatoes, carrots, sweet potatoes, rutabagas), with peas, and with their own cooked greens.

YEAR-ROUND

CARROTS	*Charcoal-Grilled Carrots*
	Carrots and Split Peas
	Carrots with Cumin
CAULIFLOWER	*Cauliflower and Yogurt Raita*
	Cauliflower Gratin
MUSHROOMS	*Wild Mushrooms with Bacon*
	Grilled Mushroom Caps
ONIONS	*"Tandoori" Onions*
	Roast Balsamic Onions
POTATOES	*Whipped Garlic Potatoes*
	Doug's Grilled New Potatoes
	Hallie's Oven "Fries"
	Classic Potato Gratin
	Potato and Leek Gratin

NOT SURPRISINGLY, we tend to prize what's rare and expensive. When it comes to vegetables, however, I think we should also prize the "workhorses" that are available in good quantity and quality throughout the year—carrots, mushrooms, onions, potatoes, cauliflower. In my mind, the vegetables in this chapter are no less appealing because they are common. Like all vegetables, they reward thoughtful attention in purchasing and preparation; even plain buttered carrots can be a delicious side dish if the carrots are truly sweet, the butter fresh, and the cooking careful.

But because they're so familiar, I often try to give these vegetables a little twist to make them new and tempting. Have you ever grilled carrots, red potatoes, or whole mushroom caps? Grilling brings out their natural sweetness and turns these "common" vegetables into uncommon dishes. Sometimes, all it takes is an unexpected flavor—like cumin with carrots (see page 197) or roasted garlic in whipped potatoes (see page 214)—to kindle interest in a vegetable dish.

CARROTS

Thank heaven for carrots. They're plentiful and cheap year-round, naturally sweet and nutritious, quick to clean and cook. With little effort, the humble carrot can make some distinguished side dishes.

Like beets and sweet potatoes, carrots are routinely oversweetened in American recipes. No amount of brown sugar or orange marmalade will make an inferior carrot into a sweet one; it only adds calories and masks the true carrot taste. Better to put your efforts into finding good carrots, or growing them yourself; sweet carrots need only a pinch of sugar, if that, to heighten their flavor.

TO SELECT
Young, slender carrots are usually the sweetest and least likely to have a woody core. Carrots should be firm, not flabby, and have full orange color with no whitish areas. The stem end should be fresh looking, not dark and discolored. Avoid horsey, overgrown carrots or carrots with cracks in them. Most carrots are sold "clip-top"—with the feathery tops removed. Some markets leave the tops attached; if the tops are in good condition, you know that the carrots have been recently harvested. Specialty produce markets sometimes carry baby carrots in bunches; if they look firm and fresh, they will probably be sweet.

TO STORE
Carrots are relatively good keepers. Remove the tops, if any, and place the carrots in a perforated plastic bag. Refrigerate in the vegetable crisper for up to 2 weeks.

COOKING TIPS
Boiling or Steaming Peel large carrots and cut them into pieces of the desired size; baby carrots do not need to be peeled, just scrubbed. Boil carrots in salted water or steam them in a steamer basket over boiling salted water until tender. Check doneness with a small sharp knife. Steamed carrots should be patted dry before dressing. Drain boiled carrots well, then return them to the pot and place it over low heat. Shake the pot until the carrots are thoroughly dry.

Braising You can braise whole finger-sized carrots or larger ones cut into small pieces. Place them in a skillet with melted butter, a pinch of sugar, and just enough water to keep them from sticking to the pan. Cover and braise over moderately low heat, shaking the pan occasionally and checking to see if more liquid is needed. By the time the carrots are tender, the juices in the pan should be reduced to a sweet glaze.

Grilling I hope the recipe below will convince you to try grilled carrots. They are wonderful.

CHARCOAL-GRILLED CARROTS

You won't believe how good these are. Grilling caramelizes the carrots' natural sugar and seems to intensify their flavor. They are also unbelievably easy to do if your fire is right. Serve with a charcoal-grilled pork tenderloin and some wilted greens, or with grilled poultry and an assortment of grilled vegetables. Thanks to my friend Sharon Thomas for this idea.

Serves 4

> **4 to 6 carrots (see Note)**
> **1 tablespoon olive oil**
> **Kosher salt**

1. Peel the carrots and carefully cut them in half lengthwise. Set them on a platter and toss them with the olive oil and salt to taste.

2. Prepare a moderate charcoal fire in a covered grill. Cluster the coals on one side so that you have an area where the carrots can cook by indirect heat. Cook the carrots, cut side down, directly over the coals until nicely browned. Watch carefully; they can burn quickly if the fire is too hot. If you sense that the fire is too hot, remove the carrots and wait until the fire burns down a little more. If the fire is at the proper temperature, the carrots will brown in about 10 minutes. Turn them cut side up and set them on the other side of the grill to cook by indirect heat. Cover the grill and cook until the carrots are barely tender, about 15 more minutes. Serve immediately.

NOTE: Buy carrots small enough to look attractive on a dinner plate. With medium-size carrots, two halves will make a serving. With small carrots, allow three.

Grilled Mushroom Caps (page 206),
Charcoal-Grilled Carrots, and Doug's Grilled New Potatoes (page 215)

CARROTS AND SPLIT PEAS

If you like split pea soup, you will love this dish; it's a ribsticking stew that calls for many of the same ingredients. Pair it with sausage, pork chops, meat loaf, ground lamb kebabs, or braised lamb shanks. Like many legume dishes, it reheats well, but take care not to overcook the peas.

Serves 4

> **8 ounces carrots**
> **2 tablespoons butter**
> **½ medium onion, finely chopped**
> **1 clove garlic, minced**
> **1 cup green split peas, rinsed**
> **1 cup chicken stock**
> **1 bay leaf**
> **1 clove**
> **Salt and freshly ground black pepper**

1. Peel the carrots and discard the tips and tops. If your carrots are large, cut them in half lengthwise, then cut crosswise at half-inch intervals. If they are small, just cut them crosswise every half inch. The goal is to end up with pieces of approximately equal size.

2. Melt the butter in a heavy 10-inch skillet over moderately low heat. Add the onion and saute until it softens, about 5 to 10 minutes. Add the garlic and saute until fragrant, about 1 minute. Add the split peas and stir to coat them with butter. Add the chicken stock, bay leaf, clove, and 1 cup of water. Bring to a simmer, then cover, reduce the heat, and simmer 10 minutes. Uncover, add the carrots, and stir once with a fork. Cover and cook until the carrots and peas are tender but not mushy and the peas just start to break down, about 20 minutes. The peas should be soft with just a core of firmness. Uncover, raise the heat to moderately high, and cook until most of the excess liquid has evaporated. The mixture doesn't need to be totally dry, but it shouldn't be soupy. Season to taste with salt and pepper; discard the bay leaf and clove. Transfer the stew to a warm serving bowl.

CARROTS WITH CUMIN

Cumin, garlic, lemon, and coriander work magic on carrots. Try them with pork chops, roast chicken, or a lamb stew with a Moroccan flavor.

Serves 4

> **⅛ teaspoon cumin seeds, or more to taste**
> **1 pound carrots**
> **1 tablespoon extra virgin olive oil**
> **1 clove garlic, peeled and halved**
> **½ cup water**
> **½ teaspoon sugar**
> **Salt**
> **Lemon juice**
> **1½ tablespoons chopped fresh coriander (cilantro)**

1. Put the cumin seeds in a small dry skillet and set it over moderately low heat. Cook, shaking the skillet often, until the seeds begin to smell fragrant and darken slightly, 1 to 2 minutes; do not allow them to burn. Transfer the seeds to a mortar and pound them to a powder, or grind them in a spice grinder.

2. Peel the carrots; remove the tops and tips. Cut the carrots into small pieces of approximately equal size; the exact size is not important as long as the pieces are equal. I usually start at the root end, cutting straight across at ½-inch intervals; when the carrot gets thicker, I cut it in half lengthwise and continue cutting across at ½-inch intervals. At the top, where the carrot is thickest, I may quarter it before cutting across.

3. Combine the carrots, olive oil, garlic, water, and sugar in a medium saucepan. Bring to a simmer over moderately high heat, then cover and reduce the heat. Simmer until the carrots are tender, approximately 15 minutes. Test often. When the carrots are just tender, uncover the pot, raise the heat, and allow any excess liquid to evaporate. Stir in the cumin and salt and lemon juice to taste. Add the coriander and toss with a fork, then transfer the carrots to a warm serving bowl. Include the garlic if you have any garlic lovers at the table.

OTHER SERVING SUGGESTIONS

HERBED CARROTS Dress boiled or steamed carrots with butter or olive oil; toss to coat. Season with lemon juice and herbs. Dill, chives, chervil, mint, tarragon, or coriander would be a good choice.

ROASTED CARROTS Place chunks of peeled carrot around a chicken or roast to cook in the roasting juices. Baste occasionally to keep them from drying out.

CAULIFLOWER

Young cauliflower has a mild cabbage taste that can nevertheless accept strong flavors. For recipe ideas, I find foreign cooks more inspired than Americans. Indians prepare cauliflower with tomatoes, ginger, mustard seed, and hot peppers; Italians with garlic and pecorino cheese; the French with chopped egg, butter, and capers. Its cabbage-like flavor also suggests some of the seasonings you might use with cabbage (fresh dill, paprika, sour cream, or yogurt) or broccoli (capers, anchovies, Parmesan cheese, and garlic).

Lifting vegetable techniques and ideas from other cultures can expand your repertoire almost without limit. In the case of cauliflower, you'll find it a much more versatile and appealing vegetable than American cookbooks lead you to think.

TO SELECT	Choose firm, compact, creamy white heads. Avoid those with a lot of brown spots. Cauliflower should smell sweet and fresh, not strong.
TO STORE	Store cauliflower in the refrigerator crisper in a perforated plastic bag. Use it within 2 to 3 days.

COOKING TIPS   ***Trimming***   You can cook cauliflower whole or you can break it apart into large or small florets before cooking. In either case, wash it well and remove the leaves, if desired. (The leaves are edible and tasty; work them into the recipe if you like.) Remove the thick base of the cauliflower with a small sharp knife, then, if you wish, cut the florets away from the stem.

Cooking It Whole   Trim away any rough parts on the base of the stem and cut an "X" in it to allow heat to penetrate faster. Boil the head in a large quantity of salted water until a small knife slips easily into the thick part of the stem. A 1½-pound cauliflower will take about 10 to 15 minutes. Be careful not to overcook it; like all members of the cabbage family, cauliflower gets an objectionably strong flavor if cooked too long. Drain well.

You can also steam the whole head over, not in, boiling salted water, although steaming takes longer. A 1½-pound cauliflower will take about 20 minutes.

Cooking Florets   Boil the florets in a large quantity of salted water or steam them over, not in, boiling salted water in a covered steamer until crisp-tender.

CAULIFLOWER AND YOGURT RAITA

Indian cooks make a tremendous variety of vegetable-and-yogurt salads, only a few of which make their way onto Indian restaurant menus in this country. Typically the vegetables are fried with spices, then stirred into room-temperature yogurt. My friend Niloufer Ichaporia, who grew up in Bombay, introduced me to this technique, which works with zucchini or onions, too. Try the cauliflower version with grilled lamb chops or pork chops or grilled chicken rubbed with Indian spices.

Serves 4

> 1 medium cauliflower (about 1½ pounds)
> 2 cups plain yogurt (see Note)
> 1 jalapeño chile
> 2 tablespoons vegetable oil
> 1 teaspoon whole mustard seeds
> 1-inch piece fresh ginger, peeled and grated or very finely minced
> ½ cup water (approximately)
> Salt
> 2 tablespoons coarsely chopped fresh coriander (cilantro)

1. Separate the cauliflower into bite-size florets. Set them aside. Put the yogurt in a medium bowl and whisk until smooth. Remove the jalapeño stem and halve the chile lengthwise. Remove the seeds if you prefer a milder dish; otherwise, leave them in. Slice each half lengthwise into fine julienne strips.

2. Heat 1 tablespoon of oil in a large heavy skillet over moderate heat. When the oil is hot, add the mustard seeds. The seeds will immediately begin to pop and splatter; use a pot lid, if necessary, to protect yourself. Add the chile and ginger, reduce the heat to medium-low, and cook, stirring, for 3 minutes. Immediately add the entire contents of the skillet, including the oil, to the yogurt and stir to blend.

3. Heat the remaining tablespoon of oil in the same skillet over moderately high heat. Add the cauliflower. Do not stir for at least a minute to allow the cauliflower to brown on one side. Then stir and continue cooking, adding water a tablespoon or so at a time as needed to prevent the cauliflower from sticking. The cauliflower should cook to the crisp-tender stage in about 10 minutes and require only about ½ cup of water. Season to taste with salt as it is cooking.

4. Transfer the cauliflower to the bowl with the yogurt; stir to blend. Taste and reseason. Serve at room temperature, garnished with coriander.

NOTE: Whole-milk yogurt will make the richest and best tasting raita, but you can use lowfat or nonfat yogurt if you prefer.

CAULIFLOWER GRATIN

This crusty, crunchy gratin needs a "saucy" main course, like braised pork or veal in tomato sauce or roast leg of lamb with pan juices. You can use either Parmesan or pecorino cheese; I prefer to use a blend of the two to get both the nuttiness of the former and the sharpness of the latter.

Serves 6

> ¼ cup olive oil
> 1 medium cauliflower (about 1½ pounds)
> Salt and freshly ground black pepper
> 2 cups soft fresh breadcrumbs
> ¾ cup grated Parmesan and/or pecorino cheese
> 2 tablespoons minced parsley (optional)

1. Preheat the oven to 425°. Choose a baking dish just large enough to hold the cauliflower florets in one flat layer; it's best if the dish has low sides. Oil the bottom and sides of the dish liberally with 1 tablespoon of the olive oil.

2. Remove the cauliflower leaves and trim the florets off of the thick stem, leaving the florets in large pieces. Steam the florets over (not in) simmering water for 3 minutes, just to moisten them; they should not be anywhere close to done as they will continue to cook in the oven. Cut the large florets into small florets and arrange them in one layer in the baking dish. Season with salt and pepper.

3. Combine the breadcrumbs, cheese, and parsley. Pat the mixture into an even layer over the cauliflower, pressing it into place with your hands. Drizzle the surface with the remaining 3 tablespoons of olive oil. Baking until well browned and crusty, about 30 minutes.

OTHER SERVING SUGGESTIONS

CAULIFLOWER TOPPINGS Spoon any of the following toppings over boiled or steamed cauliflower for a quick and tasty side dish:
- Olive oil warmed with minced garlic, anchovies, capers, and parsley.
- Melted butter, chopped hard-cooked egg, capers, and parsley.
- Breadcrumbs toasted on a baking sheet, then tossed with olive oil or melted butter and minced fresh herbs (parsley, dill, chives).

BRAISED CAULIFLOWER Braise florets in tomato sauce or in chicken stock then shower them with Parmesan cheese.

MUSHROOMS

Mushrooms are not technically vegetables; they're fungi, not plants. Nevertheless, I've included them because they often take the role of a vegetable in our menus.

The mushroom market has changed so much in the last few years that it is hard to make generalizations. The common white button mushroom that was for years the only mushroom of any commercial importance in this country has now been joined on produce shelves by many others—some cultivated, some wild. Shiitake (*Lentinus edodes*), enoki (*Flammulina velutipes*), oyster mushrooms (*Pleurotus ostreatus*), and blewits (*Clitocybe nuda*) are among those that are now successfully cultivated. What's more, many markets carry truly wild mushrooms, harvested by foragers. Here, caution is essential; wild mushrooms can be lethal and no system yet exists to license foragers. If you are interested in buying and cooking wild mushrooms, the best approach is to teach yourself to recognize the edible ones. The second-best approach is to buy only from a knowledgeable produce vendor whose judgment you can trust.

The result of all this mushroom activity is that we cooks have a lot more choices. Each kind of mushroom has its own distinct texture, shape, and taste. Some are earthy, others nutty; some are velvety smooth, while others have tiny crinkly pockets that seem designed to trap butter or cream sauce. Wild mushrooms, a spontaneous gift of the earth, have an alluring scent of mystery. They can be prohibitively expensive if you don't harvest them yourself, but I still sometimes splurge on a handful of morels or chanterelles; even mixed with a larger quantity of cultivated mushrooms, their earthy, woodsy flavor comes through.

TO SELECT   When buying the common white button mushroom (*Agaricus bisporus*), look for tightly closed caps with no gills showing. The caps should be smooth, unblemished, and firm, not spongy. Other mushrooms should be firm and slightly moist — not limp, damp, or soggy, and not dried out. The cleaner they are, the less time you will have to spend cleaning them.

TO STORE   Mushrooms get soggy if stored in plastic bags, and they don't store well in any case. Try to use them the day you buy them. If that isn't possible, refrigerate them in paper bags. If they are very moist, arrange them on a paper towel-lined tray in a single layer and cover them with a towel.

COOKING TIPS   ***Cleaning***   Cultivated mushrooms are usually pretty clean and require only a brushing with a damp paper towel; do not submerge them in water. Trim off the ends with a small knife. Wild mushrooms should be carefully brushed clean with a dry mushroom brush, an old toothbrush, or a damp paper towel. Only if you can't get the dirt off any other way should you put the mushrooms in water, and then only briefly. Blot them dry immediately afterwards.

WILD MUSHROOMS WITH BACON

The secret to success with this dish is not to rush it; stew the mushrooms slowly and they will brown beautifully all over without any added liquid. Serve them with steak, veal chops, baked chicken breasts, or salmon fillets.

Serves 4

> **1 pound wild mushrooms (see Note)**
> **4 thick slices meaty bacon (see Note)**
> **Salt and freshly ground black pepper**
> **1 large clove garlic, minced**
> **2 tablespoons minced parsley**

Clean the mushrooms with a damp towel and/or a mushroom brush. Slice them about ¼ inch thick. Cut the bacon crosswise into 1-inch lengths. Render the bacon pieces slowly in a large skillet; just before they begin to crisp, transfer them to paper towels with a slotted spoon. Pour off all but 2 tablespoons of the bacon fat. Add the mushrooms and salt and pepper to taste. Saute slowly until the mushrooms are tender and beautifully browned, about 20 to 30 minutes. Add the garlic and saute until fragrant, about 1 minute. Return the bacon to the skillet to rewarm. Remove the pan from the heat and stir in the parsley. Taste and reseason if necessary. Serve immediately.

NOTE: Use meaty mushrooms like chanterelles (*Cantharellus*) or boletes (*Boletus edulis* — what the French call *cèpes* and the Italians call *porcini*).

NOTE: If you can't find thick-sliced bacon, ask a butcher to slice slab bacon about ¼ inch thick.

VARIATION: To make this dish with cultivated mushrooms, buy 1½ pounds of cultivated agaricus mushrooms with large, firm, white caps and no gills exposed. Wipe them clean with a damp cloth and slice them about ¼ inch thick. After rendering and removing the bacon pieces from the pan, pour off all but 2½ tablespoons of the fat. Raise the heat to moderately high and add the mushrooms and salt and pepper to taste. As they cook, they will give up quite a bit of liquid, then they will start to stew in their own juices; turn them occasionally by shaking the skillet. After 25 to 30 minutes, they should be a beautiful golden brown. Continue the recipe as above.

GRILLED MUSHROOM CAPS

Imagine a thick grilled ribeye steak with a few of these juicy mushrooms on top and a bottle of your best Cabernet Sauvignon. To round out the meal, add Extra-Crusty Spinach Souffle (page 185) or Broccoli and Potato Puree (page 147).

If you have room on your grill you can, of course, cook the mushrooms right alongside your steak or any other grilled meat. If not, cook the mushrooms first and set them aside, then reheat them briefly on the grill after you've taken the meat off.

Serves 4

> 3 tablespoons olive oil
> 1 tablespoon red wine vinegar
> 2 cloves garlic, finely minced
> ½ teaspoon minced fresh tarragon
> Salt and freshly ground black pepper
> 12 large, firm white mushroom caps (about 14 ounces; see Note)

1. Whisk the olive oil, vinegar, garlic, and tarragon together in a large bowl. Season highly with salt and pepper.

2. Wipe the mushrooms clean with a damp cloth; trim any stems down to about ¼ inch. Put the mushrooms in the bowl and toss to coat them with the seasonings. Let stand 30 minutes.

3. Prepare a medium-hot charcoal fire. Place the mushrooms rounded side down over the coals and grill, turning them once, until they are an appetizing golden brown on both sides and cooked through, about 12 minutes.

NOTE: This dish requires large, beautiful, unblemished mushroom caps. Check the underside of each to make sure the cap is tightly closed; if the gills are starting to show, the mushroom is too old.

OTHER SERVING SUGGESTIONS

BRAISED MUSHROOMS Slice or quarter mushrooms and braise them in butter or oil. You can then add them to any number of vegetable dishes. For example, layer them with sliced potatoes when making potato gratin, or toss them with cooked fava beans, lima beans, or peas. Chopped cooked mushrooms are a great addition to creamed spinach.

MUSHROOMS AND PEARL ONIONS Braise quartered mushrooms in butter with pearl onions.

STIR-FRIED SHIITAKE MUSHROOMS WITH SNOW PEAS Stir-fry sliced shiitake mushrooms and snow peas in peanut oil.

MUSHROOMS IN TOMATO SAUCE Halve mushroom caps and braise them in your favorite tomato sauce.

HERBED MUSHROOMS Saute a mixture of several types of mushrooms in butter or oil and season with minced herbs—thyme, rosemary, tarragon, dill, parsley, or savory.

ONIONS

Yellow onions, white onions, red onions, green onions—all are available year-round in good quantity and reasonably good quality. Most yellow, white, and red bulb onions are dried somewhat after harvest to reduce the moisture content so they can be stored for months without deteriorating. Sweet onions are the exception; Vidalia, Walla Walla, and Maui onions, prized for their sweetness, are sold immediately after harvest, without drying. They are available only in summer because they do not store well. Green onions (also called scallions) are young bulb onions harvested before the bulb develops. Small, young bulb onions—about 1 to 1½ inches in diameter—are sometimes sold as "boiling onions." The true pearl onion is not a bulb onion (it's *Allium ampeloprasum*, not *Allium cepa*) although some marketers sell very small bulb onions as pearl onions.

Which types are best for which uses? Sweet onions—Vidalias, Walla Wallas or Maui onions—are for eating fresh, in an onion and tomato salad, on a hamburger, sliced into rings and arranged atop marinated green beans or beets. Green onions aren't as sweet but they are mild; I use them when a delicate onion flavor is most appropriate, usually adding them at or near the end of the cooking time. They need only brief cooking to release their fragrance. I rarely use red onions for cooking because they lose their color with heat. Between white and yellow onions, it's a matter of taste. I find yellow onions a little sweeter, white onions a little sharper, more "onion-y." In vegetable dishes, I prefer the taste of yellow onions, but white onions will work just as well.

TO SELECT	Onions should feel firm and dry, with bright, crackling skins. Avoid sprouting onions or any with soft or sooty parts, which indicate decay. Green onions should have dry, fresh-looking green leaves and a firm white section. Reject any that feel slimy or limp.
TO STORE	Bulb onions and pearl onions should be stored in a cool, dark, dry place in loosely woven or open-mesh bags; they will keep for a few weeks. Green onions should be refrigerated in a plastic bag and used within 4 to 5 days.
COOKING TIPS	***Bulb Onions*** To peel a bulb onion, slice off the stem (sprouting) end, then cut the onion in half through the root. Peel back the papery outer layers. Keep the root end intact to hold the onion together while you slice or chop it.
	Pearl Onions To peel pearl onions, blanch them for 30 seconds in boiling water, then drain. Peel while hot; the skin will slip off easily.
	Green Onions Trim away the root end before slicing or mincing green onions. Most recipes call for the white and pale green parts only; the dark green part is tough and strong-flavored.

"TANDOORI" ONIONS

Have you ever tried those wonderful thick-sliced onions served with tandoori dishes in Indian restaurants—the ones that come to the table sizzling on a hot iron platter? Here's my version, recommended with hamburgers, lamburgers, grilled sausages, or just about anything cooked outdoors.

Serves 4

> 2 medium yellow onions
> 1 tablespoon peanut oil
> ¼ cup coarsely chopped fresh coriander (cilantro)
> Salt

1. Cut off the stem ends of the onions. Cut the onions in half through the root end. Peel each half, then cut it crosswise into ¼-inch-thick slices. Separate the slices into individual half-rings.

2. Heat a large cast-iron skillet over high heat until very hot. Add the oil and swirl the skillet to coat the bottom and sides. When the oil is shimmering but not yet smoking, add the onions all at once. Let them sizzle for half a minute or so to brown the ones on the bottom, then stir. Continue to cook, stirring occasionally, until the onions are lightly charred and just slightly limp. They should still have a little firmness but their crispness and raw heat should be gone. Add the coriander and salt to taste; toss, then transfer to a warm serving platter.

ROAST BALSAMIC ONIONS

I like to take these beautiful onions on picnics because they travel so well and taste good at room temperature. The slow cooking enhances their natural sweetness, and a brush of balsamic vinegar near the end of the cooking time adds a sweet/sour tang. Note that the onions should cool about 45 minutes before serving.

Serves 4

> **2 large yellow onions, unpeeled**
> **4 teaspoons unsalted butter, plus more for the baking dish**
> **Salt and freshly ground black pepper**
> **8 teaspoons balsamic vinegar**

1. Preheat the oven to 350°. Halve the unpeeled onions through the root and stem end. Cut a thin slice off the rounded side of each half so that it will sit upright in a baking dish.

2. Butter a baking dish just large enough to hold the onions; arrange the halves cut side up in the dish. Season with salt and pepper, then put a teaspoon of butter on each half. Cover the dish tightly and bake until the onions are tender, about 50 minutes. Uncover and sprinkle each onion half with about 2 teaspoons of vinegar; use a fork to spread the onion layers apart so that the vinegar can dribble down between the layers. Return the dish to the oven uncovered; bake 15 minutes. Set aside and let the onions cool to room temperature before serving in their skins.

OTHER SERVING SUGGESTIONS

ONIONS BAKED IN THEIR SKINS Bake whole yellow onions in their skins in a buttered baking dish. Bake at 375° until tender when squeezed, about 1¼ hours. Split them in half and season with butter, salt, and pepper.

ROASTED ONIONS Peel and halve onions and arrange them around a roast or covered pot roast, alone or with other root vegetables, to cook with the meat.

FRIED ONIONS Slice onions and fry them slowly in a skillet or on a griddle until limp; serve with liver.

BRAISED PEARL ONIONS Peel pearl onions and slowly braise them in a covered skillet in butter with a little sugar. Pearl onions can also be blanched and then added to vegetable stews or simmered in cream with peas.

POTATOES

The plain old potato isn't so plain anymore. Thanks to increased interest in both old and new varieties, well-stocked produce markets now carry red, white, yellow, and blue ones, ranging from the size of a marble to a one-pound russet. Some varieties, such as German fingerlings, are as creamy as custard, while others such as Russet Burbanks, are as dry and fluffy as cotton. The flavors and textures are so varied, and the uses so many, that I could happily eat potatoes every night of the year.

TO SELECT   Whatever their type, potatoes should be firm and free of cuts, blemishes, or sprouts. Avoid potatoes with green areas, which are a sign that they have been exposed to light too long. Try to buy potatoes of approximately the same size so that they will cook evenly. For boiling or sauteing, choose moist, waxy-fleshed potatoes such as red potatoes, thin-skinned white potatoes, or German fingerlings. Mealy-fleshed russets are the most popular choice for baking and deep-frying, but you should also try baking some of the yellow-fleshed potatoes like Bintje, Yukon Gold, and Yellow Finn. They have a delicious buttery quality to their flesh and need little in the way of seasoning. For gratins, use waxy potatoes.

TO STORE   Potatoes should be stored in a cool, dark, dry place; they will keep for a few weeks.

COOKING TIPS   **Baking**   Russet potatoes are never better than when baked directly on the rack of a hot (450°) oven. Don't wrap them in foil or they will steam. A 12-ounce potato will be crisp outside and fluffy inside in about 1 hour. Slit it open and season it with a nugget of butter and some salt and pepper. None of the many toppings that you see served on baked potatoes these days is, to my taste, an improvement on this basic recipe.

Sauteing   Slice or dice waxy potatoes and saute them in olive oil or clarified butter. They do not need to be peeled but they should be rinsed and dried thoroughly after cutting up to keep them from sticking to the pan. Season with salt and pepper and cook over moderately high heat, shaking the pan almost constantly, until they are cooked through. Add finely chopped parsley at the end.

WHIPPED GARLIC POTATOES

These aren't mashed potatoes; they're whipped, which is what makes them so luscious. The amount of milk and cream you'll need will vary with the type of potato; the cup called for here should be plenty, and you may not need it all. Alas, this is a last-minute dish and it does not wait once made. Serve with roast pork, meat loaf, braised short ribs, leg of lamb, or the Thanksgiving turkey.

Serves 4

> **1½ pounds russet (baking) potatoes**
> **10 cloves garlic**
> **½ cup milk**
> **½ cup heavy cream**
> **6 tablespoons unsalted butter (room temperature)**
> **Salt and freshly ground black pepper**

1. Peel the potatoes and place them in a large pot with enough salted water to cover them by several inches. (If the potatoes are large, cut them in half; otherwise, leave them whole.) Bring the water to a boil over high heat. Partially cover the pot and lower the heat to maintain a slow boil. Cook until the potatoes are tender (a knife will slip in and out easily). Depending on their size, this may take 15 to 30 minutes. Drain the potatoes and return them to the pot. Place the pot over the heat again and shake it until all the water has evaporated.

2. While the potatoes boil, peel the garlic and halve the cloves lengthwise. If there is a green sprout in the center of a clove, lift it out. Place the garlic, milk, and cream in a small saucepan. Bring it to a simmer, cover, and reduce the heat to the lowest possible setting. Simmer 20 minutes.

3. Remove the garlic with a slotted spoon; put the potatoes and garlic together through a food mill or ricer set over a mixer bowl. Using the whisk attachment on an electric mixer, whip the potato/garlic mixture at medium speed, adding the butter a tablespoon at a time as you whip. When the butter has melted, turn the mixer to low and add a little of the hot milk/cream mixture. Raise the speed to medium until the liquid is incorporated. Repeat with the remaining liquid, adding it on low speed, then raising the speed to whip it in. Depending on the dryness of the potatoes, you may or may not need all the liquid. The potatoes should be very, very creamy—and remember, they will thicken slightly when you stop beating them. Season generously with salt and pepper.

DOUG'S GRILLED NEW POTATOES

My husband does most of the grilling at our house and this dish is his invention. A few minutes over a hot grill gives these oil-rubbed potatoes a crusty browned exterior. They would be compatible with almost anything, but we make them most often when we're cooking something else on the grill, like fish or lamb chops. They can cook right alongside.

Serves 6

> **2 pounds waxy new potatoes**
> **2 tablespoons olive oil**
> **Coarse salt**

1. Scrub the potatoes, then place them in a large pot with enough cold salted water to cover them by 1 inch. Bring the water to a boil over high heat, then reduce the heat and simmer until the potatoes are just done. Cooking time will depend on potato size, but a potato that's about 2 inches in diameter will take about 20 minutes. Check by lifting one out with a slotted spoon and slipping a small knife in and out. Don't overcook them or they will fall apart when you try to slice them. Remember that they will continue to cook as they cool. When the potatoes are done, drain and let them cool.

2. Prepare a hot charcoal fire. When the coals are ready, slice the potatoes in half lengthwise and toss them in the olive oil; season to taste with salt. Put the potatoes cut side down over the coals and cook until they are nicely browned, about 3 to 5 minutes. Move them around with tongs to hotter or cooler parts of the grill as necessary to make sure they brown evenly. Turn them over and crisp them a little on the skin side, about 3 minutes, then transfer them to a warm serving platter.

HALLIE'S OVEN "FRIES"

My friend Hallie Harron taught me how to make these fat "fries," which are actually baked until they're crisp and brown. They absorb a lot less oil than French fries do and are less bother, too. Serve them anywhere you'd serve French fries—with hamburgers, roast chicken, grilled fish, or a thick steak. If serving them with fish, omit the cheese.

Serves 4

> **3 small russet potatoes (about 8 ounces each)**
> **¼ cup olive oil**
> **Coarse salt**
> **Freshly grated Parmesan cheese (optional)**

1. Preheat the oven to 450°. Scrub the potatoes well but do not peel them. Cut each potato in half lengthwise, then cut each half lengthwise into three equal "fingers." Immediately place the potato wedges in a large bowl of cold water. Swish to remove the surface starch, drain, and cover them again with cold water. Let stand 10 minutes. Swish the potatoes once or twice, then drain them in a sieve under cold running water to wash away any surface starch. Dry them thoroughly in a clean dish towel.

2. Preheat a heavy baking sheet in the oven for 5 minutes. Toss the potatoes in the olive oil, then arrange them on the baking sheet, one cut side down. Season with salt. Bake 20 minutes, then remove from the oven. Using tongs, turn the potatoes over so that the other cut side is down. Season with salt. Return them to the oven and bake until they are nicely browned on the bottom, about 15 more minutes.

3. Using tongs, transfer the potatoes to paper towels to drain, leaving any excess oil on the baking sheet. Transfer the hot potatoes to a warm platter and shower them with grated Parmesan.

CLASSIC POTATO GRATIN

There's no better match for grilled leg of lamb than a creamy potato gratin. Unlike the leek- and cheese-flavored version on page 219, this one is purely sliced potatoes baked in rich reduced cream.

Serves 6

> 1½ **pounds waxy potatoes**
> 3 **cups milk**
> 1 **large shallot, finely chopped**
> 1 **large clove garlic, minced**
> **Salt and freshly ground black pepper**
> 1¾ **cups heavy cream, or more if needed**

1. Preheat the oven to 325°. Peel the potatoes and slice them about 1/6 inch thick. Put them in a 4-quart saucepan with the milk, shallot, garlic, 1 teaspoon of salt, and several grindings of pepper. Bring the mixture to a simmer over moderately high heat, then reduce the heat and continue simmering 5 minutes.

2. Remove the pan from the heat. Carefully lift the potato slices out a few at a time with a slotted spoon, letting the excess milk drain off; it's okay if a little milk clings to the slices. Arrange the potatoes in an oval gratin dish, approximately 13 × 8 × 2 inches, salting and peppering the layers as you go. (See Note)

3. Pour 1¾ cups of cream over the potatoes. The cream should cover the top of the potatoes; add more if necessary. Bake until the potatoes have absorbed the cream and the top of the gratin is beautifully browned, about 65 to 70 minutes. Let the gratin rest 15 minutes before serving to allow the flavors to settle.

NOTE: Do not discard the milk. Cool then refrigerate it. The next day, cook some diced potatoes in it, and add some shrimp, corn, ham, or canned clams for a delicious chowder.

POTATO AND LEEK GRATIN

I know you shouldn't count calories when you make a potato gratin, but this version really is relatively low-cal. It contains only enough butter to grease the dish and considerably less cream than most. Nevertheless, it's remarkably creamy, the cream infused with the lovely sweet flavor of leeks. Enjoy it with grilled leg of lamb or a fresh pork leg cooked on the grill.

Serves 6

> 1 garlic clove
> 1 teaspoon butter
> 1½ pounds red-skinned potatoes, peeled and sliced ⅛ inch thick
> 1½ cups minced leeks, white and pale green parts only
>   (2 to 3 medium leeks sliced thinly crosswise then minced)
> Salt and freshly ground black pepper
> ½ cup heavy cream
> ½ cup chicken stock
> 3 ounces grated Gruyere cheese

1. Preheat the oven to 325°. Cut the unpeeled garlic clove in half. Rub the bottom and sides of an earthenware or ceramic oval gratin dish (approximately 13" × 8" × 2") with the cut clove. Let the garlic juices dry, then grease the dish with the butter.

2. Arrange one-third of the potatoes in the dish; top them with half the leeks. Season with salt and pepper. Add another third of the potatoes, then the rest of the leeks. Season again with salt and pepper. Top with the remaining potatoes. Season with salt and pepper.

3. Whisk the cream and chicken stock together and pour them over the potatoes. Cover the dish with aluminum foil and bake 30 minutes. Uncover. Press the potatoes down lightly with a spoon and baste them with some of the liquid so that the surface is moist. Raise the oven temperature to 375°. Sprinkle the surface of the potatoes evenly with cheese. Return the gratin to the oven uncovered and continue baking until it is well browned, about 25 to 30 minutes.

OTHER SERVING SUGGESTIONS

TWICE-BAKED POTATOES Slice large baked russets in half. Carefully scoop out the flesh and mash it with butter, salt, and pepper. Add just enough hot milk or cream to give the potatoes a smooth consistency. Spoon the seasoned flesh back into the skins, top with grated cheese, and return the halves to a 350° oven until the cheese melts, about 15 minutes.

POTATOES BAKED WITH HERBS AND GARLIC I like to coat whole, unpeeled waxy potatoes with olive oil and put them in a covered casserole with some thyme or rosemary sprigs and whole unpeeled garlic cloves. I bake them in a 375° oven until a knife can be slipped in and out of a potato easily. My husband likes to put a little white wine in the dish so that the potatoes steam; that's good, too.

PAN-ROASTED POTATOES Choose small waxy potatoes. Rub their skins with olive oil and roast them whole in an uncovered roasting pan at 425° with sprigs of herbs scattered about. Or tuck them around a roast so that they cook in the roasting juices; baste occasionally.

BOILED POTATOES When you can get small new potatoes, boil them in salted water until they are just tender, then dry them by shaking them in a dry skillet over heat. Add a knob of butter and shake the pan until they are coated, then add salt, pepper, and parsley. You can do the same thing with larger red potatoes; before you boil them, peel away a ½-inch-wide strip of skin around the middle, just for looks. Boiled potatoes can also be halved or quartered and added to a vinaigrette made with lots of chopped parsley, a little tarragon, and some shallots or garlic. Toss and serve while the potatoes are still hot.

INDEX

223

Metric Conversion Table

Follow this chart to convert the measurements in this book to their approximate metric equivalents. The metric amounts have been rounded; the slight variations in the conversion rate will not significantly change the recipes.

Liquid and Dry Volume	Metric Equivalent
1 teaspoon	5 ml
1 tablespoon (3 teaspoons)	15 ml
¼ cup	60 ml
⅓ cup	80 ml
½ cup	125 ml
1 cup	250 ml

Weight	
1 ounce	28 grams
¼ pound	113 grams
½ pound	225 grams
1 pound	450 grams

Linear	
1 inch	2.5 cm

Temperature	
°Fahrenheit	°Celsius
155	70
165	75
185	85
200	95
275	135
300	150
325	160
350	175
375	190
400	205
450	230

Other Helpful Conversion Factors

Sugar, Rice, Flour	1 teaspoon = 10 grams
	1 cup = 220 grams
Cornstarch, Salt	1 teaspoon = 5 grams
	1 tablespoon = 15 grams

OTHER COOKBOOKS AVAILABLE
FROM HARLOW & RATNER

EVERYBODY'S WOKKING by Martin Yan

Companion book to the ever-popular public television series "Yan Can Cook." A 176-page quality paperback with 35 pages of stunning color photos. Everybody's favorite Chinese cook, Martin Yan makes healthful Chinese cooking simple and fun.

ASIAN APPETIZERS: EASY, EXOTIC
FIRST COURSES TO DRESS UP ANY MEAL by Joyce Jue

More than 60 easy-to-prepare dishes that fit nicely into Western menus. The recipes are drawn from China, Thailand, Korea, Japan, Vietnam, Singapore, Indonesia, and the Philippines. Quality paperback, 132 pages including 30 full-page color photos.

Jay Harlow's BEER CUISINE: A COOKBOOK FOR BEER LOVERS

Much of the world's best food goes very, very well with beer. This exuberant collection offers 78 recipes ranging from snacks and nibbles to elegant dinners for company. A few recipes use beer as an ingredient. Includes a summary of beer history and a guide to styles of beer. Quality paperback, 132 pages, including 30 full-page color photos.

HARLOW & RATNER was founded in 1990 to publish high quality cookbooks that are as authoritative and useful as they are beautiful. All of the authors published under the Astolat Books imprint are accomplished professional cooks and cooking teachers. Recipes are true to their ethnic origins and easy to reproduce in the average home kitchen. Astolat Books are for anyone who loves to cook and wants to learn from the best.